WENGER

Praise for *Wenger: The Legend*

'Gripping... Jasper Rees talks to those who know [Wenger] best – players, coaches, and the people of the village in Alsace where he grew up.'

– Guardian

'Anybody who wants to understand the modern English game needs to understand Wenger and how he has done it. Jasper Rees has done a thoroughly professional job... [He] avoids the usual football clichés and suffuses his book with humour.'

– The Times

'Rees is diligent in his research, travelling to Alsace to meet old friends and colleagues of Wenger, and there are good exchanges with Nick Hornby and Tony Adams.'

– New Statesman

'Intriguing... The story has its roots in Alsace, spreads through France and Germany, sidetracks to Japan and finally explodes in England... as good as it is because it has been researched by obtaining unprecedented access to Wenger's circle of friends and colleagues.'

– ArsenalWorld.co.uk

'I found the book to be enjoyable and informative. It paints a picture of Wenger as someone who has dedicated his life to football and is an intense competitor. He is portrayed as a sensitive, intelligent man of the upmost propriety.'

– ArsenalAmerica.com

WENGER
The
LEGEND

First published in 2003 by
Short Books
3A Exmouth House
Pine Street
EC1R 0JH

This updated paperback edition published in 2014

10 9 8 7 6 5 4 3 2 1

A CIP catalogue record for this book is available from
the British Library.

ISBN 978-1-78072-219-1

Printed and bound in Great Britain by
CPI Group (UK) Ltd, Croydon, CR0 4YY

This book is dedicated to
Alex, Pascale and Florence.
And to Gabriel Warren and Sam Denny.

INTRODUCTION

'You are not God when everyone says you are, and
you are not miserable when everyone says you are.
The truth is somewhere in between.'

Arsène Wenger

And then there was one.

In August of 1996 Arsène Wenger arrived in
London from footballing outer space – the provincial
Japanese city of Nagoya. In the rapid to-and-froing of
modern football, the year belongs to the Premiership's
Palaeolithic era. Back then there was still a considerable predominance of English players in English football, and a boy called Giggs was a gangly youth.
France had yet to win the World Cup (or New Labour
a general election). And on the north bank of the
English Channel, nobody in football chomped on
broccoli.

Results matter in all sport, but in none more than
in the billionaire's playground that is Premiership
football where the game's bosses almost always favour
the quick fix over the long view. That is why Arsène
Wenger at the start of his seventeenth season found
himself by some distance the longest-serving manager

in English football. He was ten years ahead of his nearest rival.

Compare the through-put of managers at rival clubs in England and the rest of Europe in the time Wenger has been at Arsenal. Not including interim caretakers, Manchester City have had sixteen managers and Chelsea twelve while Tottenham welcomed their eleventh through the revolving door. Real Madrid have had seventeen coaches, Juventus fourteen, AC Milan twelve, Barcelona ten and Bayern Munich nine. AS Monaco, the club where Wenger spent seven seasons, have had eleven. That's a lot of different hands he's shaken at the final whistle. The numbers change all the time, like the meter in a taxi.

Only one face was a solid factual certainty in Wenger's changing world. Alex Ferguson – latterly Sir Alex – and Wenger were there every August, and still there every May, for seventeen long years. Players came and players went (with the exception of Giggs), but their managers stuck around. Ferguson's job security was underpinned by winning things – not only all those Premierships, but the Champions League, twice.

The story is rather different with Wenger, and that is the story this updated biography will tackle in a new final chapter. It's the story of a man who has been overtaken by his own revolution but who, now that his ancient rival has finally consented to retire, may be on the cusp of starting another one.

Throughout much of their history Arsenal had offered a tough, uncompromising, rather monotonous brand of football. Before Wenger, generations had grown up on it, put up with it, got used to it. It was what they knew. George Graham in particular regimented Arsenal into practitioners of something you'd never catch Pele praising, let alone playing. It was the polar opposite of the beautiful game: it was the dutiful game. By the mid-1990s, Arsenal were as widely unloved as they had ever been. Fans were giving up their season tickets in droves. And yet within three weeks of Wenger's first training session – it was that quick – Arsenal were passing the ball on the floor for the first time in living memory. Slowly he changed everything else. He drew on the accumulated knowledge of 25 years' experimentation and research in French football, putting it all into practice. He signed foreign players the opposition found difficult to handle, played new signings out of position. He altered the eating, drinking and sleeping habits of the players he inherited, improved training routines and training facilities. And it worked. Boring boring Arsenal were transformed overnight into scoring scoring Arsenal. It took Wenger slightly less than two years to win the Double, and within a few more his ideas about match preparation had seeped into the thinking of every club in the Premiership. Then he won the Double again. He became, unarguably, the single most influential figure in English football. No wonder the Queen awarded Wenger an honorary OBE in her 2003 birthday honours list, to go with his Légion d'Honneur.

When this biography was first published in 2003, the Wenger narrative was already a thing of wonder. A year later, when it was updated for the paperback edition, Wenger and Arsenal had made history in a way no one would have predicted – or no one but Wenger himself. The previous summer Manchester United had spent around £30 million of their huge gate receipts and Asian merchandising income over the close season. This was when £30 million was a lot of money even in football. But that same summer Chelsea had begun operating under the new owner-ship of Russian oligarch Roman Abramovich, who in the close season casually wrote out cheques totalling somewhat over £100 million. The new era of football-ing hyper-inflation was launched. Wenger counted out the coppers to acquire one German goalkeeper to replace the irreplaceable Seaman. This was football as meekonomics. Arsenal then went on to do something unimaginable: to play a whole Premiership season without losing a single game. The team became known as the Invincibles.

Since then, what? Wenger has been anointed coach of the decade by a federation of football statisticians. He has had an asteroid named after him. He has also troubled the front end of the newspapers with an extramarital affair with a French rapper. But there has been only one trophy since the Invincibles - yet anoth-er FA Cup, in 2005.

In the meantime, Arsenal left Highbury, their ground of 93 years, and moved into the magnificent custom-built stadium with its lucrative 360-degree ring of hospitality boxes. The Emirates was built to house larger crowds paying more money (the most in the Premiership for a season ticket) to shrink the fiscal distance between Arsenal and richer rivals. The club came within fourteen minutes of entering their new home as European champions. Arsenal played their last game at Highbury on 6 May 2006 and ten days later were in Paris for the Champions League final where that same German goalkeeper – Jens Lehmann – was sent off after eighteen minutes and Barcelona eventually overhauled Sol Campbell's surprise goal with two of their own.

The Invincibles began to break up. Wenger had always been astute in letting his charges go when he was good and ready and had, in his view, got the best out of them: Petit, Overmars, Vieira, Henry, Pires, Gilberto Silva, even Anelka (whose legs worked rather better than his brain). The money was always used to rebuild. But the first worrying sign of a new order came soon after that Paris final. With his best years still to come and at the end of a tawdry tapping-up saga, Ashley Cole, who was one of Arsenal's very few locally sourced English successes, took the petro-roubles on offer at Chelsea. In due course other top players would leave for bigger-spending clubs: Hleb, Song and finally Fàbregas to Barcelona, Flamini to AC Milan, Nasri to Manchester City, Van Persie to Manchester United. Where once Wenger had counted on his own mystic aura to ensure loyalty, it became clear that Arsenal were no longer able to keep their best players. They became the best selling club in the country, probably in Europe and perhaps even the world.

In 2009, upon outstripping Herbert Chapman as the club's longest serving manager, Wenger conceded that he had been a reckless appointment. 'At that time, what Arsenal did, you needed to be a little bit crazy. Crazy in the sense that I had no name, I was foreign, there was no history. They needed to be, maybe not crazy, but brave.'

After 2005 a different sort of bravery was required: to stick to Plan A when Plan B – reckless spending – was seen by many as the only way to end the drought. Finishing in the top four became the new grail. An annual set of news stories took on the formal pattern of a ritual dance. The football pages would report that Wenger was confident his top player would be persuaded to stay with Arsenal. His top player would then leave. Wenger would reassure fans that he would be making a big splash before the transfer window closed. One or two signings would duly arrive that had an underwhelming flavour. It was a mixed comfort to see the return of old players whom Wenger, a great believer in youth, had allowed to leave: Lehmann, Campbell, Henry. There was even talk of bringing back the original talisman Vieira. Over the years, that degree in economics from Strasbourg, which slightly awed everyone in 1996, started to look like the cause of all the problems. As the composition of the Arsenal board was changed by death and infighting, and all sorts of heavyweights and high-rollers jostled for control of the club's future, Wenger's diligent concern about the balance sheet found him refusing to spend money the club didn't have just to keep up with the big spenders.

'To rebuild, that's exciting as well,' Wenger once said after another pillar of the team left to win things elsewhere. These words will not have been exciting to Arsenal fans after nearly a decade on a diet of jam yesterday and jam tomorrow. Rebuilding, as ever for Wenger, revolved around scouting the world for talented youth. By the summer of 2013 a minority of fans were calling more loudly than ever for Wenger to go. There was the unignorable nadir of losing 8-2 at Old Trafford. But then he went and spent £42.5 million on a single player, Mesut Özil, breaking the club's own transfer record by £30 million. The sight of Wenger throwing his money around made the entire football world do a double take. A similar *volte face* in relation to wealth spending takes place in a famous Christmas story by Charles Dickens.

But this is a new era. Liberated and perhaps even reborn after the departure of Ferguson, could this even be a new Arsène Wenger, the grand old man of English football seizing the day?

YOUTH

'I don't remember when I first kicked a football. I'm sure it was just an ordinary day for a French child, but I suppose I must have been about ten or eleven. Today, I'd say that's too late to become a first-class professional player, but I didn't know that at the time. It is a fact that from the moment I started football, I was totally engrossed in this game. Then, however, unlike today, there was a big gap between being engrossed in football and becoming a professional player. I am very doubtful that I ever felt like aiming to become a professional. Of course, that doesn't mean I never dreamed of it if the chance came up, but I didn't see football as a job. It was virtually impossible in the village where I lived to become anything like a professional footballer. In those days, there was no question of even the fairly big clubs putting effort into scouting, so nobody noticed boys playing football in a small village.'

Arsène Wenger

Every career in football kicks off with a discovery, with a discoverer. In the beginning there was Max Hild. Or 'Max' Hild. He is actually a Raymond, but he picked up the nickname while doing his military service and it stuck. Only his wife calls him Raymond. The whole of French football knows him as Max.

The young Arsène Wenger was found by Hild one spring in the late 1960s. 'He was 18,' says Hild, 'and playing for his village. I was coach for the neighbouring team. Our *espoirs* were playing against Duttlenheim. It was a Wednesday evening. I can't remember the score but we won.' The neighbouring team was AS Mutzig, a club with a reputation under Hild's stewardship for playing the best amateur football in Alsace. The *espoirs* were the kids, the ones who still have hope.

It was so long ago that England were world champions. Arsenal, with a team containing Pat Rice, Bob Wilson and George Graham, would not win the Double for another couple of seasons. Rice would later be Arsène Wenger's assistant, Wilson his goalkeeping coach. Graham would be his predecessor, and his antithesis. 'That was the first time I noticed him,' says Hild. 'He was a midfielder. He played very well. He made such an impression that I got in touch with him and the next year he came to play for Mutzig in the third division.'

Max Hild, the small trim boyish man who meets me at the station in Strasbourg, is almost two decades older than Wenger. It is a freezing Saturday morning in February and the city, the designated capital and centre of Europe, is quiet. Hild is wearing blue jeans, a tie and a navy blue jacket.

'Ponchour,' he says, in a high voice.

It takes a while to decode the inflections peculiar to

Max Hild's French. He speaks precisely, but with an Alsatian accent in which consonants melt in the mouth like butter in a saucepan. Bs become Ps, J becomes Ch, Ds become Ts. It's the accent specific to a region where the natural frontier with Germany – the Rhine – is only a few kilometres east of the city.

We get in Max Hild's car and head for a place he calls 'Tuttlenheim'. It is a cloudless day; a wintry haze smothers the Rhine basin in silence. Somewhere out beyond these intensively farmed flats are the Vosges mountains, but you can't see them, not in this opaque light. The only features to interrupt the horizontal monotony of the landscape are farm silos and the upward thrust of an occasional church.

Duttlenheim materialises like a ghost. Naturally it's the church of St Louis that shows itself first, a monstrous assertion in the middle distance. We turn off the motorway and are soon ambling along a main drag flanked by a mixture of solid modern houses and charming older structures. A settlement has been here since Roman times, and the name Duttlenheim has been around since at least 992. It feels as if some of its buildings have too. Alsatian architecture, even in Strasbourg, is at the bijou end of rustic. There are cross-hatched timber beams everywhere; every second building is a barn of some sort. There are yards with neatly piled firewood and museum-piece agricultural instruments. In one courtyard is an old wooden farm building, and a couple of tractors. Next door to it is a house, neat, modern and impeccably bourgeois with a steep sloping roof and a large conifer on the front lawn. The plate on the letter box says 'A. Wenger'. 'A' in this instance stands for Alphonse.

Further down on the same block, just by the cross-roads, is a restaurant. A bistro, they call it here. La Croix d'Or, it says above the door, not to be confused with the village's other restaurant, La Couronne d'Or. Arsène Wenger's father Alphonse ran an automobile spare-parts business in Strasbourg, but he and his wife Louise also owned and ran La Croix d'Or. It must once have been a residential house and at some point transmogrified into a watering-hole. On a blackboard outside the dishes of the day are listed. On Fridays they serve *rosbif*.

In the 1950s the Wengers actually lived in the smaller neighbouring village, Duppigheim, but they spent all their time here. It was in this building that the future manager of Arsenal grew up, along with his older sister and brother. You wouldn't guess to look at it from the outside, but within its four walls Arsène Wenger imbibed one of the central tenets of his foot-balling philosophy: that it is an offence to be drunk in charge of a football, or even to let alcohol touch your lips as a player. Perhaps 'imbibed' is the wrong word.

'When he was little he was in La Croix d'Or all the time,' says Hild, who at the end of a long career as an amateur in the lower divisions had his first drink of beer at 36. 'He saw a lot of people drinking, and the after-effects.'

In 1996, when Wenger was revealed as the new manager of Arsenal, he inherited a captain in the early stages of recovery from addiction to alcohol. Never in a rush to volunteer much about himself, it took Wenger two years to open up to Tony Adams and pool his memories of the alcohol abuse which, for better or worse, helped to plump the family coffers. 'It's further down the road that he actually had compassion for it,' recalls Adams. 'Later on down the line he shared things with me. He talked about being brought up in a Strasbourg pub and observing the way alcohol changed people, the effect the drink had on people.'

The French don't use the term, but when all's said and done, La Croix d'Or is indeed a pub. The interior is all bright pine panelling. A bar, robust and square, dominates the main room. There are tables and chairs, table football, a small dining-room off the side and a blue-and-white tiled room at the back leading to the toilets. At Saturday lunchtime it is empty. The place looks pretty much as the Wengers left it over 20 years ago. So says the current owner from under his thick grey moustache. There used to be the inevitable barn flanking the building, but that's gone now.

Later in the afternoon it will fill with the smell of cigarettes and choucroute and beer and the chatter of Duttlenheimers whose families have known and intermarried with one another in this small community for centuries. You can't imagine an environment more alien to the clean, antiseptic worlds which Wenger would later try to create at each of the clubs where he was made coach: smoke-free, alcohol-free, fat-free. And yet it was the *siège* of FC Duttlenheim – the HQ, the head office – where the talk was all of football, where the game leaked into the marrow of the young Arsène and stayed there.

On the bar is a copy of *Alsace Foot*, a weekly newspaper that gives some idea of the local passion for the game. There are 80,000 registered players in Alsace, out of a population of only 1.5 million.

'Alsace has always been football country,' says Max Hild. 'It's been the number one sport since I was a boy.' The front page of *Alsace Foot* is usually devoted to Racing Club de Strasbourg, the big city outfit, but further in the font size gets smaller and the games more local. The results of the Ligue d'Alsace, in which FC Duttlenheim plays, are noted in the back half. Village football was truly a humble launchpad for the journey that followed – to running the Prince's team in Monaco, Toyota's team in Japan, and on to the most traditional old club in the country that gave football to the world. No wonder, as the russet-cheeked barman says, while drying a glass, 'Arsène really is a hero of Duttlenheim.'

Then he adds. 'Me, I prefer fishing to football.'

Max Hild's car turns right at the solitary traffic-light and treads gently through the village. Duttlenheim has swollen, mostly at the edges, since the late 1960s when there were 1,500 inhabitants. These days there are 2,500, and a new school, better facilities. If it's quiet now, it must have been even quieter then.

We pass La Couronne d'Or, pass the ugly 19th-century bulk of St Louis (Catholic, of course), pass the *mairie*, and more barns and bungalows until we turn right down a track that leads to the sports field. At the far end there is a man-made rectangle of water for those who prefer fishing, and there are newish tennis courts. But the main facility is a small football pitch. It is hemmed in by the road on this side and the backs of houses on the other. Wedged in between the houses and the touchline is an open-sided stand of the kind you might erect to give horses shelter in a windy field.

There is no seating, no rudimentary terrace. You could cram perhaps a hundred spectators in there, but you'd have to put the tall ones at the back.

It was here, on this ground, that Arsène Wenger learnt how to play football. There wasn't a lot else to do in Duttlenheim in the 50s and 60s. For the younger children, primary school was in the village. It was run by the church. The teacher was called Sister Joseph. The cleverer ones went to secondary school in Obernai, about 10 kilometres away by bus, while the others stayed behind to learn a trade.

Wenger was one of the cleverer ones. But after school, at weekends, in the holidays, there was football, or watching football. The FA Cup final was the first foreign football he clapped eyes on, on the one television set in the village, in the school, in the late 50s. He would have seen Tottenham win one half of their double in 1961.

The children would count the cars which occasionally passed through the village. 'One of you took the Citroëns, the other took the Renaults,' remembers Claude Wenger, who may or may not be a relative. ('Perhaps our grandparents were cousins,' he says vaguely.) Everyone knew one another. 'Back then no one went away on holiday. We were together the whole time.'

Because the Wengers ran a restaurant, they couldn't always keep an eye on their children. It was a village where everyone took care of the young. Wenger later compared it to a kibbutz. But it was a Catholic kibbutz. The young Arsène put his faith at the service of the team. He'd be in church reciting from his prayer book when the team were playing on Sunday. He would pray for them to win.

When he wasn't praying, he was rounding up boys to play in the game. In such a small village, it wasn't easy getting 11 together in one age group. Arsène would spend the whole week assembling a team. Otherwise they'd have to play one short, or two. Perhaps it was in the early 1960s that he began his love affair with pace and power, as you needed these to combat numerically superior teams. Arsenal often thrive when one of their number has been sent off; and struggle, by contrast, when they are playing against ten.

Not that, at the age of 12, he could muster much in the way of pace or power. Hild says the player he later spotted was 'quite quick'. Claude Wenger says he was 'quite slow'. Most people seem to agree with Claude Wenger. He was also short enough to have earned a humiliating nickname. When he arrived at Arsenal they called him Clouseau because there was something haphazard and clumsy about him (plus he spoke English with a hilarious French accent). Then they called him Windows because he wore glasses. But as a young teenager they called him *Petit*: Titch.

'Even at 12 he was a very calm, very lucid player,' says Jean-Noël Huck, who played for Mutzig. The same age as Wenger, he came up against him throughout their teens. 'He was always the technician, the strategist of the team. He was already getting his ideas across, but calmly.' With a larger pool to choose from, Mutzig always won their games against Duttlenheim, all the way through the age groups.

Wenger was going through a growth spurt when he got into the FC Duttlenheim first team at 16. When he shot up, he still didn't use his head much, or at least not in the air. Training was once a week, on Wednesday evenings. There was no coach as such to instil tactics and skills, but someone who oversaw the session. On the pitch, even as the youngest player in the team, Arsène was in charge. 'He was virtually, more or less, *le patron*,' says Claude Wenger. 'Arsène wasn't the captain and yet he was. It was, "You do this, you do that, you do this, you do that." He was the leader.'

Arsène Wenger was born in October 1949, two years after his older brother Guy. The three Wengers all ended up playing together for Duttlenheim. Guy was left back, Claude was right back and, according to Claude, Arsène was not a midfielder but an old-fashioned inside right. He also disputes Hild's suggestion that Arsène was 18 when he was discovered.

'He was spotted by Max Hild on 6 May 1969,' he says. Which makes it a Tuesday, incidentally, not (as Hild says) a Wednesday. Arsène was a few months shy of 20. 'He played his last game for us on June 22, 1969, against Dannemarie in the Haut-Rhin, and we became champions of Alsace.' The history books record that they actually became regional third division champions.

What Hild does remember correctly is that the young Arsène was the best player in the side. 'He was head and shoulders above his team-mates and I sensed that he had the potential to go further.' The further he went in football, so the joke took root in Duttlenheim that actually Hild picked the wrong Wenger.

'Now when the old guys talk about it they still say that Guy was better at football than Arsène,' says Claude Wenger, who chuckles at a popular local witticism for what must be the umpteenth time. 'That makes us laugh because if you had a meeting at two in the afternoon his brother would turn up at half past. Arsène was always early. Guy was 100 per cent the opposite to Arsène. Guy had one small fault. He liked going out in the evenings. Arsène was extremely serious.'

Roger Niggel, who is now the mayor of Mutzig, remembers playing against both of them. 'Arsène's brother didn't have his outlook or his technical gifts. He was a bit more hot-headed, a bit less methodical.'

Even at that age of experimentation and discovery, Arsène wasn't a drinker. 'Drink wasn't our style,' says Jean-Noël Huck. The most they'd ever treat themselves to was *un panaché*, a shandy. At 16 or 17 Wenger and Huck started hanging out together on Sunday evenings if the games weren't too far away. Their two areas of study were football and girls: there was a lot of theory, but also some practice.

In the days before the discothèque came to rural Alsace, they would go to village dances and local fêtes. There were a couple of other friends and they started going on holiday together, to a villa on the Costa Brava, to a hotel in Rimini. They chased girls and played hours of football on the beach and went out at night. They never came in later than two a.m.

By the time Wenger started playing for Mutzig, Huck had gone to play for Racing. He introduced Wenger to two other young profes-sionals, Marco Molitor and Dario Grava. Thus Wenger found him-self in an Alsatian gang of four in which he was the only one who would not go on to play for France or even, it seemed at this point, any higher than the ama-teur third division. The three of them went to watch him play at Mutzig on Sundays. In Strasbourg they would hang out at Snack Michel, opposite the main post office. Their company was a constant reminder of his own limitations as a player. He compensated for the talent gap by bleeding his friends dry.

'He was full of questions,' says Grava, who repre-sented France at the Olympics in Mexico City in 1968. 'He asked about how selection happened, training ses-sions, physiology, muscles. He took a lot of notes. He was already more a coach than a player. At only 20!'

And he always had his sheer cleverness to fall back on. 'You could tell he was a football intellectual,' says Molitor. 'He was tuned in to everything, watching everything.' They were a bright bunch. Molitor used his spare time to do a course in physiotherapy at the university's medical faculty. Grava had left school young, although, unlike most comparable footballers in England, he read copiously: Balzac, Dumas, Voltaire.

'Arsène was quite precise in his choice of reading,' says Grava. 'He read *France Football* a lot.' But there was no escaping it. 'Of the four of us,' says Huck,

'Arsène was the only one who took his studies further. It showed in his conversation, in his vocabulary. Intellectually he was way ahead of most people.'

The fact is that if Wenger harboured ambitions to be a professional footballer, Max Hild turned up too late. He was by now at Strasbourg University doing a degree in politics and economics (having started out briefly in medicine). 'Scouting as we know it today wasn't like that in those days,' says Hild. 'Now you do training courses for youngsters of 13 or 14. Back then it wasn't as precise a science as it is now. If he had been spotted at 15 or 16, he could have had a playing career, without doubt. He could have turned into a good first division professional.'

The best Hild could offer a player of nearly 20 who was already set in his ways was a place in the first team of AS Mutzig, where Hild himself ended his playing days as a defensive midfielder – *un porteur d'eau*, in the earthy French phrase: a water-carrier. It seems Wenger's advanced age didn't matter because, even though Wenger thought about little else, he was also a pragmatist. The plan was for him to spend his life trading in automobile spare parts. 'He wasn't pre-destined to be a footballer,' says Hild. 'He was going to take over his father's business in Strasbourg after his studies.' In the end, Guy took over the family firm instead while his younger brother studied, trained and played, studied, trained and played through three clubs and ten years.

You can trace the path of Arsène Wenger the foot-baller via the size of the *tribunes* (or stands) he played in front of. Mutzig is a short drive south from

Duttlenheim. Max Hild's hatchback potters on through and almost out the other side of the town until there on the left, behind a fence, is the ground. The stand is a low structure a third of the length of the pitch. It is green, and has seating. It holds several hundred, but it was a popular team and crowds regularly reached 1500. Or the entire population of Duttlenheim. Just across the road from the stand, behind some houses, looms the red rocky mass of the Vosges foothills. They have appeared out of nowhere.

AS Mutzig was in the third division, known as the National, which was broken up into six national regions each containing 16 clubs. The eastern division was composed partly of the reserve teams of larger clubs – Sochaux, Besançon, Metz, Nancy, Racing Club de Strasbourg. Hild had been coaching at Mutzig for six years with some success. The players were amateur and trained twice a week – three times a week pre-season – and on Sunday mornings before the game met at a hotel on the corner of the main street, right under a towering medieval gateway to the old town. Wenger walked straight into the first team and stayed there.

It was a big leap from village football. 'He did incredibly well to establish himself,' says Hild, who seems to have prized Wenger's merits as a player higher than anyone else. 'His playing style was of someone very tall, long-limbed, very skilful, with a very good picture of the game. He ran a lot, he was quite quick, he passed the ball well and had good speed of thought. On top of that, he was good in the air.'

Can Hild compare his protégé to a modern player? He thinks for a bit and then plumps for Ray Parlour. About a week later he changes his mind. 'He was rather more like Roy Keane.'

From the entire history of world football, he couldn't have come up with anyone less temperamentally similar. 'He was very energetic,' explains Hild, 'a midfielder who went forward a lot, and scored goals.' But he wasn't one for premeditated revenge attacks then, or the juddering vein in the neck? 'No, he always knew how to control himself. He's always had self-control, as a player and a coach.'

Wenger stayed for three years, in which time Mutzig won the Coupe d'Alsace. The final at FC Strasbourg 06 was at Schiltigheim, a tiny ground on the city outskirts. Roger Niggel remembers 'quite a tense match', but Mutzig won 3-0. At this higher level he seems to have been less voluble on the pitch. Niggel, who was 12 years his senior, and played alongside him in midfield, says that 20-year-old Wenger 'didn't talk much. He was very calm in the matches. Maybe once or twice he'd shout. But he was very controlled. He liked winning the ball and could get forward quickly. He was a simple player. Like he is in life. He wasn't *exubérant*. He did what was asked of him.'

Wenger formed only superficial relationships with his team-mates. Dario Grava noted that he didn't thrive in new social situations. 'I wouldn't say he was closed, but he was reserved. He made friends with difficulty. He wasn't outgoing. With us, his friends, it was fine. But if someone came along that only one of us knew, Arsène didn't talk much; he was on the defensive. Maybe it was some sort of screen to protect himself. If this person came along three or four or five times, and he saw that they were at least acceptable, it would be easier for him. But he always held himself back a bit.'

What he found much easier was to place his trust in someone older than himself, someone he could look up to. This turned out to be a pattern in his life: the lure of the vertical relationship. As soon as he joined AS Mutzig a much deeper rapport with Hild took root. Hild had not just spotted a talented young footballer. He had found for himself a surrogate son, and Wenger had found a surrogate father.

'Arsène was like a son to me,' he says proudly, emphatically. 'He was at my house all the time.' Hild took Wenger fishing. Although his young friend didn't really care for it, it was a sign of his studiousness and his curiosity that he still wanted to know how the equipment worked. It's not as if Wenger's father Alphonse didn't come to all the games. But Hild and Wenger shared a common passion. Playing football was not enough. Talking about it wasn't either, although there was a phenomenal amount of that. They had to watch it too, and not just on the German television they could get in Alsace. They had to watch the best football in Europe in the flesh. At the time, that was to be found just a few hours down an autobahn over the border in West Germany.

And so it started. Three or four times a year, the odd couple – a short middle-aged man and a lanky young man – would head out across the Rhine. 'We'd arrange it for when we didn't have our own games and when the game wasn't too far away.'

Wenger had already been taken to watch Borussia Mönchengladbach as a boy by his father, though not quite enough to count himself an actual supporter. Now they cherry-picked the best games in the Bundesliga. Munich was only three hours from Strasbourg; Stuttgart was half that. Frankfurt wasn't far either. Not that they hurried home. They'd stop on the motorway on the way home to eat and talk.

'Our conversation always revolved around technique, tactics, strategy, the organisation in the game. Arsène was always searching for something. He was very receptive and was always a very good analyst of players.'

Wenger loved what he saw. 'The Germans were inspired by the attacking game,' says Hild. 'All the defenders attacked, all the time. Everyone was allowed to go forward. But everyone had to defend.' Sometimes they didn't get home till three or four in the morning.

They also went to internationals to watch a side graced by the blond-maned playmaker Gunter Netzer, the keeper Sepp Maier with his huge gloves, the Afro-haired fullback Paul Breitner, the thunder-thighed striker Gerhard Müller. It was a generation which grafted industry onto something more carefree. They rolled their sleeves up, but they also rolled their socks down.

This lasted for most of the 1970s, the decade when West German football was at its peak. West Germany won the European Championships in 1972, and the

World Cup on their own turf two years later, when they beat a gifted Dutch side. Bayern Munich, meanwhile, obliterated all before them, winning the European Cup for three years in succession from 1974, including the defeat of Leeds United in 1975.

The final was in Paris, and Hild and Wenger were there to witness the Leeds fans rip up the stadium seating and earn the club a three-year ban from European competition. (This was Wenger's unpromising introduction to English football culture.) Bayern were masterminded at the back by the Kaiser, Franz Beckenbauer, the kind of visionary *libero* on whom, in his wilder flights of fancy, Wenger modelled himself.

Twenty years later Bayern Munich would try to lure Wenger away from Monaco to become their coach. It was Beckenbauer who made the approach. Wenger has always been as scrupulous as possible about honouring contracts, and he turned the Kaiser down.

It was consistent with his personality that Wenger wasn't a noisy spectator even at the biggest games. 'He liked the atmosphere in the stand,' says Hild. 'But it wasn't him who made the atmosphere.' Did he ever get excited? 'No, never.'

The biggest trip and the biggest game came in 1977. Again it was to see a European Cup final between a German side and an English one. Bayern had been knocked off their perch, but Borussia Mönchengladbach, the team Wenger had seen as a boy, made it to the final in Rome in their stead. Their opponents were Liverpool.

This time the two Germanophiles had company: they flew down to Rome with the rest of AS Vauban, the small Strasbourg team Hild was now coaching and Wenger was playing for. It's not as if Wenger was actively a fan of Borussia. 'He quite liked Mönchengladbach,' recalls Hild. 'And we thought they were going to win.'

And when they didn't, was Wenger downcast? 'Not at all. For us it was enough to see a good game. We were neutral.' Berti Vogts had, with maximum efficiency, snuffed out the threat of Johann Cruyff in the World Cup final in 1974, but he failed to eliminate Kevin Keegan. It was seen as Keegan's greatest game for Liverpool. It was also his last: he too had decided that the best football was being played in Germany and that summer moved to Hamburg. (The European Cup was promptly won by English clubs for six years in succession. In three of those finals West Germany supplied the losers, including in 1980, against Nottingham Forest, Keegan's Hamburg.)

Only a year later Wenger's career as a footballer reached its peak when he made a solitary appearance in European competition, for Racing Club de Strasbourg. He played as a libero, the Kaiser's position. The opposing team were, inevitably, West German. It was an unmitigated disaster.

PLAYER

'I've always paid attention to others' experience. When I was 20, I would listen to my grandfather and thought he was intelligent. Now and then, he'd come out with something that I thought was stupid simply because I was young. But, as I get older, I realise that people weren't expecting me to be clever. I told myself, "Don't be stupid enough to think that anyone born before you is an idiot. Listen to other people." All great successes, all great lives have involved the coincidence of aptitude, talent but also the luck of meeting people who have believed in you. At some point in your life you need to meet someone who will tap you on the shoulder and say, "I believe in you."'

Arsène Wenger

There was a standing joke at London Colney, the Arsenal training ground outside St Albans. The players are warming up. The squad contained some of the best players in the world. Pires, Bergkamp, Henry. While they're at it, Arsène Wenger, to whom these gifted young charges profess in interviews to owe absolutely everything, decides to take a few penalties.

And yet as far as they are aware, he was a nothing player, a trundler, a carthorse, a Robin Reliant. He summons the club's travel manager and shoves him in goal. He addresses the ball. Perhaps he is wearing shorts, which by no means flatter a spindly man in his fifties. In Alsace they remember him as *longiligne* – long-limbed – but those limbs have now dwindled into pipe-cleaners. He runs up, with the slow lope of a giraffe. He is always trying little tricks. If he misses, there is derision, there is mockery, there is hooting and baying. But if he curls the ball into the top corner he turns round for a reaction, for applause, for the acclamation he never had as a player. But these World Cup winners, these European Champions, have turned their backs. There is silence.

Arsène Wenger played out his career as a footballer in something like silence. The biggest crowds he tended to come across were no more than 2,000-strong. It is now accepted in Britain that the extraordinary coaches are just as likely to have been ordinary players. See also Alex Ferguson, Ron Atkinson, Graham Taylor (at Watford in the 1980s) and, most pertinently of all, the other Double-winner at Arsenal, Bertie Mee. They have somehow alchemised their mediocrity as players into a managerial will to win. In Mee's case, he never played at all: he was a physiotherapist. This is just as true of France as it is of England. As coaches of the national team, Michel Hidalgo and Roger Lemerre both won the European Championship; Aimé Jacquet won the World Cup. Between them, they mustered a mere nine international caps. Exactly how ordinary a player was Arsène Wenger?

While still at Mutzig he was selected to represent Alsace in the annual competition between the regional leagues. There weren't many games, and he played in no more than a handful. He also strolled into the Strasbourg university side. Later, in the mid-1970s, he was picked for the national French students squad. He was mainly in the reserve side, but it was a chance to travel. The team went to Nigeria, Lebanon and, in 1976, to Uruguay, where the World Students Championship was held. France finished third. However thrilled Wenger was to be attending an international tournament, it was at least in one sense an anticlimax. He was injured for the duration. 'Instead he took on the role of assistant coach,' says Jean-Luc Arribart, who was the team captain.

The team was largely composed of students in their mid-20s finishing off their diplomas in physical education. Most of them were of sufficient standard to play in the French second division. Wenger was no different. In the summer of 1973 he and Max Hild had a temporary separation. He had made a good enough account of himself at Mutzig to be summoned into the rarefied altitudes of professional football.

Actually it was semi-professional. FC Mulhouse is the second oldest club in France (although, to be pedantic, when it was founded in 1893 Mulhouse was temporarily in Germany). In 1971, after decades in the amateur leagues, it took its place in the second division, and the club added four or five professionals to a workforce consisting largely of part-timers who earned their wages by day and came on to training in the evenings. As a perpetual student, Wenger was always one of the semis: he took a small salary of roughly 2,000 francs a month (or 50 quid a week) and carried on studying. Training was three nights a week – Tuesday, Wednesday and Thursday – and Wenger had to get on the train and make the 100km round trip down south.

Wenger's first coach there was Robert Alonzo, who had taken over halfway through the previous season and led the club to sixth, making Mulhouse the highest-placed part-time side in France. That didn't prevent the break-up of the team. In fact it hastened it. Wenger's arrival coincided with the departure of three of the professionals, who went elsewhere in search of better pay than anything a club with gates as low as 1500 could offer. Without them, it was a struggle for what was essentially a rump collection of amateurs. In 1973-4 they finished tenth, not always with the help of their studious young recruit because, even in these reduced circumstances, Wenger couldn't always count on a place in the first team.

'That first season was very difficult for him,' recalls Marc Siffert, another semi-professional who taught PE in the week. 'He didn't get into the first team that often.' He wasn't *un super-joueur*,' says Alonzo, the man who didn't pick him. 'He didn't have the ability to play as a professional.' But his frequent exclusions seem not to have frustrated Wenger. 'He was intelligent enough to understand his limitations. He integrated himself in the team despite the fact that sadly he wasn't always an automatic selection.'

Alonzo lasted into Wenger's second season at Mulhouse, only for results to tell against him. As the club flirted with relegation, he was sacked in October 1974. To replace him the directors chose the best available, certainly in Alsace. They hired a man called Paul Frantz, whose specific task was to perform a salvage operation and avoid the drop. As Frantz also lived in Strasbourg, he joined Wenger on the train. So it was that for several months Wenger found himself thrown by chance into the company of the grandfather of Alsatian football.

Frantz is, without doubt, the most respected coach Wenger ever came across. If Hild is the man who nurtured Wenger's passion for the game, Frantz was a different sort of role model. After the war he won a state bursary to attend university in Paris, captained the French students team, and then for 30 years he taught at the Centre Régional d'Education Physique et Sports (CREPS) in Strasbourg.

That was the day job. He also trained and assessed aspiring coaches at the annual three-week summer retreats organised by the Fédération Française de Football (FFF). Among the alumni to have absorbed his teachings are Jacquet, Lemerre and Guy Roux, the freakishly long-serving coach of Auxerre. He was also a club coach. Max Hild played under him at Wittisheim. For much of the 1960s he took charge of Racing Club de Strasbourg, for whom he won the Coupe de France in 1966. 'He was 20 years ahead of his time,' says Marco Molitor. While at Racing Frantz had an offer to go and coach AC Milan, whom his Racing side had beaten in the UEFA Cup. He wasn't a contract-breaker, and he turned them down. 'I didn't speak Italian,' he says, 'I think words are very important for a coach.' Like many in Alsace, he did speak German, and after Racing spent a season coaching Karlsrühe, just over the border. The regular home gate was 40,000. Getting FC Mulhouse out of a hole was a strictly temporary act of charity.

In the winter of 1974-5, Frantz was writing a theoretical book about football coaching, and used his commutes on the train to work on it. He and Wenger travelled together. He remembers Wenger as 'a very clever student: he was very obviously of above-average intelligence. One day I was processing statistical data for my book and there was something I couldn't work out. Arsène, who had time on his hands, said, "Do you want me to tackle the problem?" In five minutes – wham! – he had sorted it out. I knew he was clever, but not that clever.'

Wenger's place in the side was, according to Frantz, unassailable. But then the new coach wasn't spoilt for choice. 'He wasn't good with his left foot,' says Frantz. 'He didn't use it much. He was of average pace, and hard-working. He knew how to organise the game.' As ever, Wenger played in midfield, generally on the right flank. A new player was brought in, a Chilean called Jorge Infante. It is the first recorded instance of Wenger having any form of contact with a foreign footballer. Not for the last time, he thrived on it, and started to play better. The joy of coaching him was that he didn't need to be told twice, or sometimes even once. 'You'd put a problem to him in training and he'd solve it.' He had what Frantz calls '*un psychomoteur*': a fast brain.

And yet Frantz noted that, however theoretically intelligent Wenger was off the pitch and even on it, at this level he lacked the gifts to express that intelligence fully on the field of play. 'As a player he was a fine tactician. You could go over any footballing problem with him. But there was a sort of imbalance in him, in that on the one hand he had remarkable perception and analytical abilities, but on the other he wasn't always perfect when it came to putting it into practice. There was this discrepancy between the conceptualising of a situation and the realisation. That was his problem.'

Frantz pondered this gap between theory and application in Wenger's game, watching a player with whom he clearly bonded off the pitch falling short on it. His diagnosis was the same as Hild's. 'After a while I discovered that he had come to football rather late. There are things that you have to learn when young. He could certainly have been a very great player, but he never was. He was an excellent amateur but that was as far as he got. If the realisation had been as perfect as his vision, he would have been a great player. In the execution he was missing something: a millimetre, or a centimentre. The passes wouldn't go where he wanted them to.'

I meet Paul Frantz, a guarded and rather frail old man, in his tidy chalet-style home in Oberhausbergen, one of those Germanically named villages just outside Strasbourg which betray Alsace's ethnic diversity. *Football*, the book that Frantz wrote on the train between Strasbourg and Mulhouse, sits on the table of his open-plan dining-room. It is turquoise and dog-eared with an unrecognisable picture of the author as a middle-aged man on the cover. This is his only remaining copy. It is in the end a rather dry and extremely theoretical textbook, and Frantz himself has the air of a sort of human textbook. When he talks about the numerical composition of a football team, he does so with the help of a mathematical formula.

'A team,' he says, 'is not simply the addition of 1 plus 1 plus 1 all the way to 11. It's a multiplication.' He writes it down. $T = (1+2+3+4+5+6+7+8+9+10+11)$ to the power of n. 'N,' he explains, 'is the influence of the coach.'

Paul Frantz's ideas about football, enshrined in *Football*, had a formative influence on Arsène Wenger that it is impossible to overstate. It was Frantz who formalised his thinking on the science of nutrition, on fuelling before a game and refuelling after it, on the notion that an ill-prepared player subtracts from the overall efficiency of the team. Wenger had never been a roisterer, but Frantz says 'he listened attentively. He was open to these dietary issues. He swore by the rules on eating and drinking. They were sacred for him.' Frantz also introduced him to isometrics, a workout of short, timed exercises which build the muscles without putting any strain on a player's joints. A couple of decades later, isometrics would take the old guard at Arsenal by surprise.

Another precept that Wenger learnt from Frantz, even as Frantz practised it on Wenger, was the notion that no two players are the same. Frantz got this from attending a conference where the philosopher Albert

Jacquard was speaking. 'He said, "Each man is unique." I worked out straight away that that means each player is unique. You need above all to work with this uniqueness: to get something out of a good player, I have to recognise his strong points. I tolerate his weak points but I work with his strong points. I believe that, by working like that, Arsène sensed how to get the maximum out of Thierry Henry.'

And that is how Frantz got the maximum out of Wenger. Only the maximum wasn't quite good enough for the French second division. Was it frustrating that he didn't quite have the skill to do with his feet what he visualised with his head? 'Indisputably. We talked about it. But I didn't like to point out someone's weaknesses. You want to bring certain players up.'

In the summer of 1997, at the end of his first season at Arsenal, Wenger was invited back to Mulhouse to give a talk. Though he had fallen into the habit of spending his holidays with friends on the Côte d'Azur, each summer he would also go home to Alsace, where invitations like these turned up regularly. He'd answer questions about his childhood, his reading habits, his attachment to Alsatian dialect, his politics (he had several friends at university who were communist, but he is instinctively a pro-European centrist). Outside the shareholders meetings and press conferences, in England he never submitted himself to the scrutiny of an audience. The reason he could do it here was that the reverence, and pride in his achievements, were tempered by a characteristic Alsatian reserve. Among the guests was Paul Frantz, whom Wenger had long since replaced as the most eminent Alsatian in football. Wenger paid tribute – *'un grand hommage,'* remembers Frantz, wistfully – to the man who had filled his head with knowledge that would prove indispensable. They haven't met since. 'I will never forget our constant discussions from Strasbourg to Mulhouse,' says this small, rather melancholy guru. 'But that's life. The teacher is always overtaken by the pupil. And Arsène has really and truly overtaken the teacher.'

As Alonzo had discovered, it was extremely difficult for Mulhouse. The club struggled to keep up with fully professional clubs – including at times both Monaco and Racing, who had somehow got themselves relegated. Their squads didn't have to go to work on Monday morning. Even if the division was split geographically into east and west, it was still a long journey back from Toulouse or Cannes. It took the best part of a day to get down there by train, and a day to get back. With a day in the middle, away trips were a three-day excursion. No wonder Wenger took his studies slowly, and resorted to doing them by correspondence. Sometimes it seemed as if he spent his entire life on the train. One part of his degree that normally takes two years he took in three.

Although the dice were loaded against them, Frantz kept them up in the last game of 1974-5: they beat AS Nancy Lorraine. One of Wenger's opponents in midfield that afternoon was the young Michel Platini. Nine summers later Platini's goals would win the European Championship for France, and Wenger would begin his coaching career at Nancy. His two years at Mulhouse would represent the only experience of struggle he had to draw on. And he'd need them.

The job done, Frantz left. He wasn't alone. On top of the travelling to away games, Wenger had to throw in the commuting from Strasbourg. After two seasons it all got too much for him. Besides, in the summer of 1975 he had an offer to hitch up with Max Hild again, and this time he could go back to playing football on his own doorstep, even if it meant mingling once more with the amateurs.

In 1971 a new club was created called AS Vauban. A year earlier, an old Strasbourg club called Pierrots had merged with Racing Club de Strasbourg, to split after just one season. Pierrots renamed itself Vauban, and its directors set themselves a challenge: to get into the French third division. They had to start out in the equivalent of the tenth division, and in six years they duly climbed six divisions, finishing top each season. In 1974 they hired Max Hild, who duly left Mutzig after 12 years. He joined the club for the second half of an extraordinary run of 113 games without defeat. After a season Hild brought in Wenger. 'I lacked a midfielder who could organise play and also have a sort of hold over the team,' says Hild. Weighing up the options, Wenger found that it wasn't so difficult a choice. It may have involved plunging through three divisions to the Promotion d'Honneur, but playing for Vauban meant that he no longer had to schlepp down to Mulhouse three times a week. There was also the attraction of playing for Hild again. If he'd stayed at Mulhouse, there would have been a new coach after

Frantz's interregnum, the third in a calendar year. It wasn't as if the crowds were much bigger in the Second Division, at least at Mulhouse. Vauban attracted a gate of about 1,000, affording them, for the division they played in, proportionately deeper pockets than those of Mulhouse with their home gates of never more than 2500. And anyway, Wenger would be 26 in October 1975. His friends Jean-Noël Huck and Marco Molitor had left Racing and gone down to join Dario Grava at Nice. By this time they had all played for France. He represented the French students but Wenger knew that whatever fantasies he may once have harboured of playing at the top flight of French football would remain just that. At least in the fifth division he could be the best player on the pitch.

Vauban is a residential district on the eastern edge of Strasbourg. Germany hovers just five minutes' drive away. It's not pretty, like Duttlenheim or Mutzig. But for Wenger it was a short ride from Rue de Rome, where he lived, and not far from the university either. The ground is guarded on one side by a squadron of ugly purpose-built high-rise apartment blocks. A flyover passes along one end. The pitch itself has a stand all along one flank. The rest of the ground is open. It wasn't much different from where he'd been playing. But it turned out to be the most successful team Wenger had ever played in. Previously he had won a divisional championship in Alsace with Duttlenheim and the Coupe d'Alsace with Mutzig. But in Hild's era Vauban won three successive promotions. At one point they went 69 games without losing. Within three seasons they were in the third division.

In another part of the city, Racing Club de Strasbourg were also about to enter the most glorious three years in their history. Under Frantz in the 1960s they had won the Coupe de France and beat superior European opposition at a time when French football was a minor continental player. Then the club collapsed into the second division, came back up, went down again. In 1977 they won the second division championship. The other side to be promoted with them were AS Monaco, who promptly won the Championnat. (Those were more democratic times: in the same two seasons Nottingham Forest also followed up promotion with the championship.) The next year, it was the turn of Racing. For the only time in their history, they won the league title. Incredibly, for a player with a very modest record of bumping along the bottom of French football, Arsène Wenger played his part.

It was, admittedly, a very small part. He shouldn't really have played at all. That wasn't why he was at Racing. But there was no one else.

It happened like this. The coach of Racing was Gilbert Gress, who in the 1960s had played in midfield for France and, in the Racing side that won the Coupe, for Frantz. 'The reserve coach didn't play the same kind of football as me,' says Gress. 'I tried to come out and play a bit like Ajax. So I was looking for a replacement.'

The replacement he looked for was on the doorstep: Max Hild. 'I said, "Listen, Max, drop everything and come to Racing." It was a risk for him. He was an amateur. He thought a couple of days and then agreed.'

Hild's new job title was *directeur du centre de formation*: coach of the reserve team. But there was a problem with the arrangement. Back in the first division, they finished in third place in 1977-78, their highest finish in 31 years, and so qualified for the next season's UEFA Cup. Racing had not played in Europe in a decade, they were unfamiliar with the opposition, and Hild found himself going on the kind of reconnaissance missions that he and Wenger had been undertaking off their own bat for years.

Football clubs, especially provincial ones, employed fewer staff back then, and internal moonlighting was a necessity. When Hild was scouting or spying, it left no one to run the reserve team. 'As Max was often with me watching teams abroad,' says Gress, 'he said, "We need someone a bit older for the young players. Arsène's available."'

Gress had vaguely heard of Wenger, but didn't know much about him. 'I knew him by reputation. I didn't know him directly but I'd read about him in newspapers while I was playing for Marseille.'

But he trusted Hild. Wenger was now 28. His playing career, while an agreeable and occasionally successful diversion for someone who seemed to be turning into a career student, was in effect over. His thoughts, even if only on a subconscious level, had been turning towards coaching for as much as ten years.

It was the best offer he was ever likely to get: a full-time job – his first – at the club which, like the vast majority of Alsace, he grew up supporting. He hadn't banked on playing though, or not in the first team. He helped Hild run the reserve team, which consisted mainly of *espoirs* and senior players who were either out of form or coming back from injury.

Hild allowed one of Wenger's private fantasies to come true. He moved him from midfield to the centre of defence, and asked him to play as a *libero*: Beckenbauer's position. It was the move conventionally reserved for great midfield playmakers of a certain maturity who no longer had the legs to run the game from anywhere but the back. It was like commanding a ship from the bridge, or running a battle from a well placed hill. In years to come Giancarlo Antognoni would do it. So would Ruud Gullit. Glenn Hoddle, who was Wenger's first and most significant purchase at Monaco, ended up a sweeper too. 'Arsène had the vision to play sweeper,' says Hild. 'He had the positioning and the intelligence.'

Gilbert Gress is, in every respect, the absolute opposite of Arsène Wenger. He is loud, garrulous, emotional, open and, as his employment record suggests, never slow to pick a fight. And far more than Wenger, whose coaching successes have all been beyond local borders, he is a hero of Alsace. According to Gress, there's another difference. 'He's cleverer than me, because he's never come back to Strasbourg.'

He arrives in the forecourt of the Meinau stadium, in an airy southern suburb of the city. It was here, to this concrete bowl, that the Racing team coached by Gress lured crowds averaging 20,000 in 1978-79 – huge for a provincial French club. He pulls up in an absurdly overspecified old black Mercedes. It's a perfect fit, the car of a superannuated wide boy. (When he was a young coach at Monaco, by contrast, Wenger arrived at the training ground each morning in a Renault 17.)

Gress has overgrown white hair, frozen in the dishevelled style he must have adopted in the early 1970s, and large thick-framed glasses. He is wearing a brown leather jacket, and there is a metallic rat-a-tat to his voice.

The three French coaches who have presided over the most European games are Guy Roux, Wenger and Gress. They are all from Alsace. But only one of them has brought the Championnat to Strasbourg. We drive to a quiet café further into town. Gress has his face to the room, and several times throughout the conversation he nods at someone coming in or going out. Occasionally they greet him as Monsieur Gress. It's not as if he knows these people. But they know him. Being Alsatians, they are the model of discretion and don't actually interrupt. But on those occasions when they do accost Gress, there is only one thing they want to talk about: 2 June 1979.

As Wenger's job was to play for and help coach the youth team, at first he had virtually no contact with the *titulaires* – the first team. He certainly didn't train with them. It was a variation on the theme at Mulhouse. There he had been separated from the rest of the team by dint of geography. Now it was the talent gap which kept him apart from the first team. It was the best first team ever assembled at Racing. They were thriving in the league, five points clear at the top. This was the season in which they went 25 league games without being beaten. Things couldn't have gone any better if there hadn't been a growing list of injuries. 'At that time you didn't have 25 players,' says Gress. 'You had 16 or 17.'

They worked their way through to the third round of the UEFA Cup in November, and welcomed Duisberg over from West Germany for the first leg. The score was 0-0, a moral victory for the visitors but at least the home side hadn't shipped any goals. For the return leg, Jacques Novi was injured. Novi was a regular in the national team. He was the sweeper, the position Wenger played in the reserves. Normally Gress would have used someone else, but the injury list was too long. There was nothing for it but to ask his assistant reserve team coach to plug a hole. Thus Wenger found himself playing in the Kaiser's position, sweeper, in the Kaiser's country, West Germany. He didn't quite play like the Kaiser, though.

Gress wheezes with laughter at the memory of a game that happened a quarter of a century earlier. 'We had a lot of injuries. So we took a lightweight team with a lot of replacements. And I asked Arsène to stand in for Novi. It was winter. It was perishing. As we'd drawn 0-0 at home we had to attack to try and score. It's not an excuse but the pitch was frozen – it was practically a sheet of ice – and my boys just couldn't get that goal.' Racing, with their new sweeper commanding the defence, were obliterated: the score was 4-0. 'It wasn't Arsène's fault at all. He was an amateur. And it was a blessing in disguise. If we'd had more matches in the UEFA Cup, we wouldn't have won the title. We didn't have the squad.'

Novi didn't recover in time for the visit in early December of AS Monaco, fielding several internationals who six years later would play for Wenger or coach alongside him. Thus, after the calamity of his one and only foray into Germany with his boots on, Wenger finally found himself at the unimaginable altitude of the First Division, playing for the championship leaders against, of all teams, the champions. No wonder the *espoir* from Duttlenheim came down with an attack of breathlessness. 'That was the only time he might have had a bit of vertigo,' says Gress. 'It was stressful, an important game, a full stadium. At times he wasn't comfortable. I think he was nervous.' As well he might be. The full house was approximately ten times the size of any home crowd Wenger had played in front of. Still, Racing won.

Wenger was rarely called up after that. When Racing were champions the following season, he played in a 0-0 draw, away to Nîmes. 'Arsène had a really really good game,' says Gress. 'Every time I needed him he was there. And he didn't come to be a professional. He came to train the youth team with Max Hild. We got him in because he was *un pédagogue*.' A teacher.

ASSISTANT

'When I felt that I was reaching my own limits as a player, I became the coach of the Strasbourg youth team. In fact, my family were very strongly opposed to that. They were more shocked by my decision to become a coach than a player. A player can at least retire at 30 and take another job, but that doesn't hold for a coach. That means giving almost your whole life to football. But I was very independent, and wasn't going to consult with anyone. I decided my life for myself.'

Arsène Wenger

In 1979 Arsène Wenger played his last meaningful game of football. He was now a coach, if only an assistant, if only of a reserve team. In October he turned 30. In less than five years' time he would be at the helm of his own first division club. In less than ten he'd coach a club to the French championship. Within 20 he'd win the Double in England. It's not as if he entirely misspent his youth at a level of the game where teammates played on Sunday and went back to their offices on Monday. But playing, it is clear, was not his real vocation.

Why was Wenger the coach so much better than Wenger the player? It's simplistic to say that failure in one career created an unquenchable thirst to excel in the other. The success of any good coach goes right back to the source. The great generation of Scottish managers who dominated British football from the 1950s to the 1970s – Matt Busby, Jock Stein and Bill Shankly – all hailed from the West of Scotland coalfields. Wenger's great rival Alex Ferguson grew up steeped in the culture and ethos of the Govan shipyard. Their rivalry is founded at least in part on a cultural gulf: a proudly working-class, urban, unionised, blue-collar, early school-leaver in the case of the demonstrative Ferguson; as opposed to the repressed Wenger, who is from a rural bourgeois background, and is endlessly educated and multilingual.

One of the reasons Wenger gave for famously not staying behind for a drink with Ferguson after games at Old Trafford was that he doesn't drink whisky. (If he'd gone, he'd have found out that Ferguson always serves red wine.) It may have been a flippant remark. But they drink pale, interesting, enigmatic white wines in Alsace that a lot of people can't get on with. In short, what became of Wenger is entirely bound up in where he came from, bound up in the joke that everyone likes to crack: that he is not French at all, that he is actually, when all's said and done, a German.

The anecdotal evidence seems to bear that out. Whenever those who know him best defined Wenger as a man and a coach, it was always the same. Out came the words like a four-pronged mantra. '*Travailleur, rigoureux, droit, discipliné.*' Hard-working, strict, upright, controlled. Put like that, they do sound like a set of distinctly German virtues, rather than more extravagant French ones. His success as a coach seems to be intimately bound up in his Germanness. Which begs the question: precisely how German is Arsène Wenger?

For the answer we have to go back to Duttlenheim, through a wrought-iron gate and into the village cemetery, a serried rectangle of pristine marble graves. Here on these sturdy headstones is written corroboration of the idea that, ethnically, the village Wenger first played football for has somehow found itself on the wrong side of the Rhine. From the evidence of the surnames of the interred, the gene pool doesn't offer much of a multiple choice for prospective local breeders: there are only 12 or 15 clans to choose from in Duttlenheim. This is one of those villages where family trees more closely resemble a thicket. The same names crop up over and over. Together they sound like a Bundesliga football team: Geistel; Munch, Jungbluth, Kopp, Roth; Heckmann, Weber, Fenger, Hubscher; Denny, Wenger. Not a lot of French names there.

When the German army invaded France nine years before Arsène Wenger's birth, the northern and western half of the country was placed under military rule, while the less populous, less strategically relevant southern part was left to the control of the puppet Vichy regime. Only Alsace-Lorraine was absorbed directly into Germany: the Reich was reclaiming what it deemed its own – a *volk* who had seen the border roll back and forth across Alsace like a spring tide. It had become French under Louis XIV, then German in

1870, rejoined France in 1918 and Germany again in 1940.

After the invasion, Alsatian football clubs found themselves playing in a German league. As a result of these fluctuations, in a lot of families who called themselves French the only language spoken was German. Paul Frantz's parents were German speakers. He learnt French as a foreign language in school from the age of six; but then after 1940, when he was 13, French was banned in schools.

Max Hild's parents were also predominantly German speakers. He was seven when war broke out, and had his first French lesson after the liberation, when he was 14. 'In our hearts we are French,' says Frantz. 'We don't like to admit it,' adds Hild, 'but perhaps we are a bit German.'

Language was not the only way in which Alsace was Germanised. Young Alsatian men were forcibly recruited for the war effort. Thousands died at the eastern front in Stalingrad. Fearing conscription, many fled to Switzerland, only for their families to be interned in concentration camps. In 1944 Frantz was drafted into the Luftwaffe as a mechanic. Wenger's father, Alphonse, was also conscripted.

The memorial outside the church in Duttlenheim hints at Alsace's wartime story. It makes the same florid appeal to the emotions as any such memorial in any French village square. A statue in brown marble depicts a seated woman comforting two weeping children, one on each side. It commemorates the fallen of the village from 1914-1918, 1939-1945 and Algeria. It's noticeable that there are heraldic crests on the plinth listing the Great War victims, but none above the Second World War dead. That's because they didn't give their lives to liberate France. However reluctantly, they died fighting for the Third Reich. Of the 32 from Duttlenheim who fell in German uniform, five were Wengers.

The war left its mark on Alsace. After liberation, reintegration went haltingly. Fans greeting Alsatian footballers playing in other parts of France called them '*les boschs*': huns. When Frantz with his bursary attended university in Paris, life was 'very difficult'. Alsatians were not popular and, as a result, he says, 'Alsatians of my generation are not friendly. They are untrusting. Because he comes from a younger generation, Arsène didn't have these problems.'

Perhaps Wenger wasn't directly affected, but according to Gilbert Gress, Alsatians are never allowed to forget where they come from. 'They say that if an Alsatian wants to succeed,' says Gress, 'then he has to be clearly better than others to be recognised. Maybe less now but for a long time it was true.' Being Alsatian is a bit like being Welsh, in short, but at the very centre of Europe.

Luckily for Wenger, he was clearly better. While at Racing he started studying to get his coaching badge. Initially qualifications were regional. At CREPS in Strasbourg he did a preliminary course for coaching children, then an intensive six-day course which he had to get through to allow him to do the national coaching badge. His teacher at CREPS was Ernest Jacky, who nearly ten years earlier had picked him to play for the *espoirs* of the Ligue d'Alsace. 'He was an extraordinary boy,' says Jacky. 'He was quite a laid-back student, but he was keen to learn, and totally serious. He lived only for football.'

For the national badge he worked on his own throughout the year, in preparation for an annual residential course run by the FFF in Vichy. It took place over three weeks in the summer. There were courses in theory, and its application on the pitch. They studied tactics, individual skill, physiology, theory of refereeing, how to work on speed, how to coach a group. At the end of the stay there were exams, written and practical.

Wenger was at home at least in one sense: he had never had any problems passing exams, and football was a comfort zone for him. Yet Vichy was in many ways the worst possible scenario for Wenger. There were 150 coaches on the course, of all ages, none of whom he knew on the first visit. For someone who found it difficult to make friends there and then, as his friend Dario Grava had discovered in the Snack Michel in Strasbourg ten years earlier, there was nothing for it but to assume his default setting and clam up. There were up to 20 students to each group, and they were split alphabetically.

Wenger found himself in the same group as Philippe Troussier, who did become a friend. Years later, Wenger was asked by the Japanese FA to recommend a Frenchman to coach the national team. He suggested Troussier, who duly guided Japan as co-hosts into the second round of the 2002 World Cup.

'Even 20 years ago Arsène Wenger was someone who cut himself off from everyone else,' says

Troussier. 'I wouldn't suggest that he didn't partici-
pate in group conversations, but he was very reserved.
He didn't communicate with anyone. You never saw
his passionate side, his obsessive side. He didn't give
any outward signs of this great appetite for the game
that he has. He didn't like to show feelings. In the
end he's someone who's quite distant. No doubt that
comes from his upbringing. It's given him quite a
cold personality.'

At Vichy, Wenger was doubly isolated: by the
vague sense of separateness, if you believe Gress, that
hovers around anyone from Alsace, compounded by
his own shyness – his inability, or reluctance, to hurl
himself into the fray. But it didn't impact on his ability to learn. It probably intensified it.

Jean Petit, who was later his assistant at Monaco,
says that Wenger 'wasn't silent because he had nothing to say. He was always listening, making a mental
note of things. If he detached himself from others, it
was because he already had different ideas from the
rest of us. You wouldn't say he was more advanced,
but he was more tuned in. He saw things better.'

One thing did hold him back though: his status as
a part-timer. The system was unabashedly weighted in
favour of those like Petit who had played for France.
However close to the top of the class he was, Wenger
was still trying to learn with weights attached to his
ankles. Wenger had several friends who were internationals; his squad back in Strasbourg contained internationals at youth and junior level. On a purely technical level he probably knew as much as any international, if not more, about fitness, strategy, training

methods – all of them things on which he'd been gathering knowledge since the age of 20. Petit testifies that if professionals were struggling, Wenger knew the answer. But he had not been an international himself, or even a professional, and he was stuck in the slow stream. There are three badges in the French qualifying system. Those who'd played for France were fast-tracked straight onto the next level when they passed an exam. People like Wenger and Gérard Houllier had to wait a year or sometimes two years longer. To get to the third and highest level, it could take an amateur seven years. It was like qualifying to be a barrister, or an architect.

The system sanctioned a form of apartheid. 'The part-timer has always been slightly dismissed by the professionals,' says Frantz, who qualified among professionals, and became an instructor himself. 'It's not as if he was excluded, but as an amateur Arsène found himself on the sidelines. You don't have an inferiority complex but the instructors force one onto you.'

Back at Strasbourg, Wenger was Max Hild's assistant – and representative on the pitch – as he carried on playing in the reserve team in the third division. At the *centre de formation* they had about 18 players aged from 16 to 18. For two years Wenger was the *libero* and captain. 'He was like a big brother to them,' says Hild. 'They all listened to him. He had a gift for passing on his knowledge to others.' You sense from conversations with Hild that, in Wenger the footballer, he always saw more than others did. As the man who found Wenger and launched him on his footballing odyssey, he has a lot invested in the idea that his protégé could play. Thus Hild argues that Wenger was good with young players 'because he was an excellent player himself, and because he was still playing'.

But the fact is that Wenger was far more gifted as a teacher. It was Hild's idea to enlist him, but Paul Frantz, who was on the board of Racing at the time, had spotted his potential too. 'I told the board, "Arsène is a remarkable guy. He'd be a really ideal example for young players; he'd be like a father to them."'

And so Wenger became, if not quite a father or a big brother, then maybe an uncle to the *espoirs* of Racing: close, but also removed. The oddity was that, aside from his curiosity and his intelligence, the thing that served him so well was the very character flaw that baffled Troussier in Vichy. His diffidence may have made it hard for Wenger to open up among his peers but it made him a natural at telling people what to do. 'Even when you know him very well,' says Troussier, 'he keeps his distance. He never calls you. It's always me who makes the effort, who makes the first move, who maintains the relationship. He never goes out of his way. Why, I don't know. He's rather shy, or someone who can sort out all his own problems.'

While some old friends are frequent visitors to London, others have suffered from this tendency of Wenger's to let friendships fall away. Marc Siffert, his old team-mate at Mulhouse, and his wife were guests of Wenger at Wembley for the 1998 FA Cup Final. They have drifted apart since. Marco Molitor, one of the Strasbourg gang of four, stopped seeing Wenger in their 20s. But however infuriating this tendency may be in a friend, 'it gets interesting in a coach,' admits Troussier, who has watched Wenger at close quarters at Nancy and at Monaco. 'His reticence is quite hard to put up with. Whenever you phone him, if you don't talk he won't talk. He's like that with everyone. But it has helped him as a coach. It allows him to get a reaction out of others. He needs to be at one remove from the players. When you train very well paid top-level athletes who are trying to find out your weakness, perhaps to provoke you, you maintain your authority in the group a lot better if you keep your distance. The fact that Arsène doesn't communicate easily allows him to maintain a certain authority. You don't know too much what he's thinking or how he's going to react. It's one of the best qualities to have as a coach. It gives him charisma, puts him in a position of strength.'

In other words, Wenger has the teacher's classic psychological profile. He thrives on a close personal rapport with pupils – or in his case players – that is entirely one-way. It allows him to get to know those in his charge intimately – to ask about their home life, to do all but tuck them up in bed – without having to give anything away about himself. Alongside the ability to work hard, it was what made him such a good pupil too. He thrived on the dynamic of the vertical relationship. As a young man, he was sitting at someone else's feet. All the way through his career in France there was always an older man with whom he bonded: first Max Hild, then Paul Frantz, and others would follow. But as a coach the roles were reversed, and in the next 25 years he'd have a lot of star pupils catching pearls of wisdom at his feet. Of all of them, perhaps only Nicolas Anelka would be ungrateful.

After winning the championship in 1979, Gilbert Gress had one more season at Racing, in which he reached the quarter-finals of the European Cup before losing to Ajax. By September 1981 he had fallen out with the president at Racing. He went to coach FC Bruges, who had lost to Liverpool in the European Cup Final a couple of years earlier. There was a domino effect. That year Max Hild's first team had finished the season unbeaten in the National, the equivalent of the third division, and he was rewarded with the chance to coach the first team. So there was a vacancy at the *centre de formation*.

Wenger took charge of his own team for the first time just before his 32nd birthday. He threw himself into it: coaching in the morning, immuring himself in his office at the Meinau stadium in the afternoon, where he organised travel to away games, met parents, prepared yet more training sessions.

'He was the best coach I ever had,' says Bruno Paterno, who joined the club at 17 just as Wenger was taking over. 'His knowledge of football, his ability as a teacher, his strictness and at the same time the simplicity of his ideas. And his sense of humour.' Yes, his humour. Wenger may have presented an intense seriousness to anyone who met him for the first time, but in the safety of his own domain it turns out he knew how to have a wry laugh, as Arsenal players would later attest. However, he never allowed it to undermine his authority which, even at a relatively young age, was total. 'He was strict on the pitch,' says

Paterno. 'He was strict about training, about applying yourself, about concentrating, strict about the instructions he gave before the match.'

Everyone from Bruno Paterno to the great Enzo Scifo goes on about his strictness. This is just a theory, but perhaps it comes from a specific, unlikely source: Wenger may have subconsciously drawn inspiration as a coach from his Catholic schooling in Duttlenheim. Indoctrinating their pupils in the rigid precepts of Rome, nuns are never the most flexible teachers. The loving rod of iron turned out to be Wenger's weapon of instruction too. He wouldn't do it any other way but his own. He rewarded his young charges with continued selection if they kept the faith. And if they didn't? If they disobeyed his instructions?

'He warned us that we wouldn't get away with that sort of thing if we ever made it as professionals,' says Paterno, who like several of Wenger's old Alsatian teammates and protégés now works at CREPS. 'That's how he chose his team: he wouldn't select you to play on the Saturday, and that meant everything. You had to perform every week of the year in training. For him that was the only criterion: you applied yourself in training and you played.'

The stadium was being refitted, so the reserve team played in outlying grounds – at Elsau in the suburbs, or Lingolsheim in the countryside. They were the kind of grounds Wenger had played in all his life, and the games attracted the size of crowd he was used to. For the first season, he carried on playing as well as coaching. In 1982-3, as he edged towards his mid-30s, his long legs started to fail him and bit by bit he retreated to the bench.

Meanwhile, down in Mulhouse, age was catching up with another player who was a full four years older than Wenger. Jean-Marc Guillou joined Wenger's old club in 1982 as player-coach. He had played his last international for France, whom he had also captained, in 1978. He and Wenger met in Alsace when playing for the Variété Football Club, a sort of roving circus for superannuated players and celebrities. Guillou was the most high-profile footballer Wenger had yet befriended, and clearly he knew far more about Guillou than Guillou knew about him. They soon discovered common ground.

One of the many things they agreed on, remembers Guillou, was that the coach of a competitive side 'should never lose sight of the fact that he has an educational role, even with players who earn a lot of money or with players who are too old for the *centre de formation*. They're still young men even when they're over 25.'

For all his silver hair, Jean-Marc Guillou looks rather younger than Wenger. We meet him in his concrete bunker of an office under the stadium of KSK Beveren. Beveren is a suburb of Antwerp, and the local football team is more or less Guillou's personal fiefdom. At the time of our meeting it is the latest stop in a career which never quite evolved in the conventional manner from the pitch to the bench. Guillou got out of management relatively early and pursued his true interest, which was in developing young players in Africa, specifically the Ivory Coast. The natural progression after setting up local training schemes was to bring young players to Europe. He plumped for Belgium, which of all countries in Western Europe has immigration laws which put up fewest impediments to his scheme, and he bought KSK Beveren. In due course he and Wenger set up an arrangement between their two clubs: Beveren would become a nursery for young Arsenal players.

In Wenger, Guillou found someone who exuded the paternalism he favoured in a coach. He wasted little time in offering him a job. Guillou noted that if the Racing's reserve team coach was ambitious, 'it wasn't that obvious. I've never seen him as someone devoured by ambition. He's certainly wanted to get on, but he wasn't so obsessed by it that he'd do anything to get there. I don't think he'd try to get anywhere by walking all over other people. Guillou hatched a plan in which he wouldn't have to. Although he'd never actually watched him at work, he was sufficiently impressed by Wenger to ask him to come back to Mulhouse and coach the first team. No matter that that was actually Guillou's job. 'I wanted Arsène to be coach and I'd become the general manager.' Wenger was all for it. But there was an obstacle. 'You could tell that he was passionate and intelligent, and someone who had a good approach to the job of coaching young players and that he'd probably succeed. The problem with the president of Mulhouse at the time was that he was afraid.' Guillou was unable to convince his president and the plan came to nothing. Guillou promptly resigned, and Wenger's chance of coaching a first team would have to wait.

Not for long, though. Guillou was still determined to work with Wenger. A few months on, in the summer of 1983, he offered him another job. This time it worked, and an association began which would last for decades. The job wasn't in Alsace, where Wenger had lived for all of his first 34 years, but in the south, in Cannes.

Wenger was no stranger to the Côte d'Azur. When his friends from Strasbourg – Dario Grava, Marco Molitor and Jean-Noël Huck – were signed by Nice in the early 1970s, he regularly made trips down to visit them, mainly in the summer. 'Almost every holiday he came to stay with me in Nice,' says Huck. 'And then we wouldn't budge. He liked it in Nice.' It was on these trips that he first met one of their team-mates, Daniel Sanchez, who to this day puts up Wenger and his family at his home in Nice in the summer. (On Wenger's recommendation, Sanchez got the coaching job at Nagoya Grampus Eight a couple of years after his friend had moved to Arsenal.) Like Guillou, to begin with Sanchez detected no great ambition in Wenger. 'I never heard him say he wanted to get his badge and become a coach. Or not at once. It was hard to picture him becoming the coach he is today. He was intelligent, but you'd never have guessed.' And yet there must have been something, because Sanchez adds that 'when he began his career at Cannes, it didn't remotely surprise us. His great strength was his ability to analyse precisely. He knew exactly what went on on the pitch: what worked, what didn't. It's something that he has in himself. Either you have it or you don't. It's not in books. You can't learn it.'

Moving to Cannes brought to an end an association with Max Hild that had begun in May 1969. 'We had a good ten years together,' says Hild. 'But it was a very good thing he left here. He wanted to learn, he wanted to coach his own team. No one is a prophet in their own land. To succeed, you have to leave.'

The idea at Cannes was to start afresh with a young coaching team and win promotion to the first division. Guillou was recruited by the club's young general manager, Richard Conte. Conte had never heard of Wenger. They met at Nice airport and discussed contractual arrangements through the night. 'They were very modest terms,' says Conte. 'We couldn't make him a big offer.' Wenger signed a contract offering him 12,000 francs a month, or roughly £300 a week. Conte, who remains a friend, remembers talking on the phone with Wenger after he'd signed another contract with Arsenal. 'He said it was exactly the same process save for the difference of several noughts.'

Wenger needed somewhere to live. Conte found him an apartment in the same block as his own, in Villefranche-sur-Mer, overlooking the Mediterranean. Guillou remembers that Wenger's place was extremely spartan. 'He didn't have furniture. He had only what he needed. He didn't care about comfort. He was totally disconnected from those realities. What was important was a bed so he could sleep well. He was very pragmatic. If you have to spend an amount of time looking for nice furniture, that's time you're using up when you could be watching videos.' And that was what he spent an inordinate amount of time doing. 'Videos, videos, videos,' says Conte. 'He was always watching videos of his opponents, of his own team. It didn't matter what time of night.'

Though Wenger may have enjoyed moving to a part of France where he had been holidaying for a decade, he didn't take a less Alsatian attitude to work. He brought a little bit of Alsace into the *centre de formation* he ran. 'He was punctual, reliable, and he never let up,' says Conte. He read specialist books on musculature. He brought Paul Frantz's ideas on iso-metrics down south. 'He was a lot more interested than me in the specifics of training,' says Guillou, who found that he had employed someone with more of the qualities required for the job than he himself possessed. 'The coach is a model for the players when it comes to behaviour. Arsène is a father figure. He is very rarely at fault. He is much stricter than me. Strictness confers respect and the players end up imi-tating him.'

Wenger's only relaxation was running with Conte in the early mornings or late evenings, along the beach or in the mountains, or playing two-a-side with Guillou, Conte and Boro Primorac, a Croatian foot-baller who played in central defence for Nice and much later went on to become Wenger's closest ally at Grampus Eight and at Arsenal. The rest of the time he lived and breathed his job with a monastic zeal. Guillou claims that they talked about moral issues, philosophy, current affairs. But 80 per cent of the con-versation was about coaching, about motivational techniques. 'When you're young, you spend a lot of time looking for the best coaching methods possible, ones that will have miraculous results. We did some interesting exercises, but we didn't find them. There is no miracle.'

There was certainly no miracle on the pitch. The first team started the season badly. 'It was hard to get them to play as a team,' says Guillou. But things slowly improved. Cannes got to the quarter-final of the Coupe de France. One of the reasons for the improvement seems to have been that Guillou was away on business in Africa, trying to sign a young Ivory Coast player called Youssouf Fofana. Wenger was the beneficiary of this trip twice over. In the long run, he inherited Fofana when he took over at Monaco three years later. More immediately, it gave him the chance to run the first team in Guillou's absence. It put him in the shop window, and it didn't take him long to be noticed.

COACH

'Being a coach is always the same job, just with different people. The hardest thing is to arrive at the right time and leave at the right time. It is like a love affair – one always wants to split up less than the other, and when it is over they take longer to overcome their disappointment. There are people who keep thinking about it and chewing it over before getting on with things. There are also those who couldn't care less about it right away. That is more me.'

Arsène Wenger

On the other side of the conference table is the most recognisable face in French football. It belongs, confusingly, to a man almost no one has heard of. That's because Aldo Platini has handed on a precise imprint of his own features to his son Michel, the greatest footballer France has ever produced.

1984 was a good year for French football, and a good year for Arsène Wenger. That summer Michel Platini electrified the football world in a European Championship hosted and won by France. Meanwhile, Wenger got his own team. The idea hatched just a year earlier had been for him to stay at Cannes for the same duration as Jean-Marc Guillou. The approach from AS Nancy Lorraine came suddenly and unexpectedly. However much they wanted to keep him, no one at Cannes stood in his way.

'I didn't attempt to hold on to him because this was an opportunity for Arsène,' says Guillou. 'He wasn't the type to stay yoked to someone else, like some second-in-command. He had the substance to be a number one.'

Still only 34, Wenger may have had the substance, but at the dawn of his career as a first-team coach he wasn't seen by his new employers as a miracle cure. He got his first major job because they were desperate, and he was cheap.

It was Aldo Platini who contacted him. He is a short, genial man with the same soft eyes as his son. When he offered the tall, reserved, quietly ambitious young man the job, he can't have known that he was taking out a temporary lease on a sort of surrogate son.

'I was just his right-hand man,' he says modestly, but that is to underestimate the sort of bond Wenger liked to form with colleagues who were rather longer in the tooth. As a modest player, the fledgling coach had little to draw on by way of personal experience. But he was fuelled by an obsessional curiosity, and made a habit of gravitating towards older men. Aldo Platini was the next in line. Like Frantz and Hild, he had never risen above the status of amateur player.

We are in the boardroom of the Stade Marcel-Picot in Nancy, 150 kilometres or so across rolling farmland to the north-west of Strasbourg. The wall at one end is in fact a floor-to-ceiling window, with a fine view of the pitch. It's an enclosed little ground, slightly too grand for the modest turnover of the French second division, but then it was built at a time of optimism. Outside, the pitch still bears traces of unmelted ice from the weekend: the game the day before was cancelled. There is no money for undersoil heating at AS Nancy Lorraine.

When Wenger chose to come back north after a year on the Côte d'Azur, he was within easy visiting distance of friends from home. But it wasn't quite the same as Strasbourg. For a start they pronounced his name with a soft G, as in 'avenger'. And where the capital of Alsace had a passion for football, the capital of Lorraine did not. Nancy has never really been a football town. This isn't a formal way of measuring anything, but when Aldo Platini and I speak in the club boardroom, it is the current president who saunters in and takes our orders for tea or coffee. And then comes back with two steaming white plastic cups. It wouldn't happen in Monaco.

When France prepared to hold the World Cup in 1998, the mayor of Nancy vetoed, on grounds of cost, a bid to be one of the host venues. It is a stolid bourgeois city, quiet and slightly staid despite the plentiful presence of students. In the line of restaurants near the beautiful 18th-century main square, people drink Moselle and eat calves' heads and persist in their love affair with the florid provincial moustache.

The resident football club is young, created from the union in 1967 of the professional FC Nancy, which had folded two years earlier, and the amateur AS Lorraine. The amalgamated club promptly enjoyed its period of greatest success, thanks to the emergence of the young Platini, who was in the first team at 17. (His father followed him to the club to take charge of the *centre de formation*.) They scaled unprecedented heights, and lured crowds to match, when in consecutive seasons they reached the semi-final of the Coupe de France and finished 4th in the Championnat.

Then in 1979 Platini moved to St Etienne. His father stayed behind, as director of football, charged with buying and selling players, but not with hiring and firing coaches. That was the president's job. Over several seasons, results remained solid but gates did not, even when they just missed out on European qualification in 1983. That was the first season under a much loved ex-player called Hervé Collot. By his second he wasn't so loved. The club flirted with relegation, key players either left or didn't perform, and at the end of the season Collot resigned, citing ill health. All of a sudden there was a vacancy. 'So we didn't have a choice,' says Aldo Platini. 'We had to find someone quickly.' Many careers in football management arise from the ashes of someone else's. Wenger, also to profit from Arsenal's brutal sacking of Bruce Rioch after only a year in charge, was no different.

As has been the case with Wenger wherever he has gone, nobody knew much about him when he took up his new post. People had to take it on trust that he was as good as the recommendations seemed to suggest. His praises were sung to the president, Gérard

Rousselot, by an old Nancy player called Jean-Claude Clouet who had fetched up at Cannes. Rousselot had no idea who Wenger was. 'But Aldo Platini knew him very well,' he says. Actually, he didn't. Beyond seeing Wenger play for Strasbourg's reserve team, Platini didn't know a great deal about Wenger either. But the recommendation came from the most enthusiastic source: Max Hild. 'It was through the intercession of Max that Arsène came to Nancy. He told me he was a good coach. We didn't know, because he was coaching only at reserve-team level.'

Platini met Wenger in Cannes, which he was visiting anyway on the look-out as usual for cheap young players. 'We hit it off, and I asked him if he'd be interested in coming to Nancy. It wasn't usually my role to contact coaches, but I did that time. Normally it would have been the president. But he trusted me.' Wenger came up to Nancy for contractual negotiations with Rousselot, and duly signed a three-year contract worth roughly 25,000 francs a month, or about £2,500. 'A coach didn't earn that much back then,' says Rousselot.

By the time Wenger took over, the triumphs of the mid-1970s were quietly fading and the money was running out. With Michel Platini inimitably running the midfield, the club had drawn average gates as high as 13,000 (and that is huge for Nancy). In Wenger's first season, even though it turned out to be his best, they were down to below 6,000. Without gate receipts, there were fewer funds to strengthen the squad, or persuade leading players to renew their contracts. And Nancy never spent more than they actually had in the kitty. Wenger's first job in the spotlight was going to be a struggle.

The problem with a reserve team is that its successes on the pitch are secondary to a distant goal. A reserve team is a nursery. Whatever you plant there, it flowers elsewhere. There's nothing ultimately to win, nothing at stake. At Strasbourg and Cannes, Wenger was in effect pottering about in the greenhouse. Now for the first time he found himself coaching a team where results at the weekend actually mattered. Without significant funds to rebuild the squad in his image, he had to hunt around.

It was here that he initiated a shopping technique which would become familiar to Arsenal fans. Deploying a mixture of instinct, improvisation and blind, sometimes misplaced faith, he played the footballing markets. He secured a Portuguese defender on loan from Paris Saint Germain, and a centre forward from neighbouring Metz in the fourth division. (Much later he'd try, and fail, to sign Robert Pires from there for Monaco.) In one of those strictly speculative punts that will (or possibly won't) evoke vague memories of the hopeless David Grondin and the hapless Igor Stepanovs, he gave a debut to a forward called Samuel Lobé, who played 12 times for Nancy in four seasons and ended up hopping from club to second division club.

But Wenger also needed someone he could trust, a pair of eyes and ears on the pitch, just as he had been for Hild at Vauban. To replace the club's long-serving sweeper Philippe Jeannol, who was lured away by the glamour and money of Paris Saint Germain, he contacted an old friend, Jean-Luc Arribart. An unspectacular footballer, Arribart had spent his career with unspectacular clubs – Rennes, Laval, Stade de Reims – as well as playing for the French students, which is how Wenger had met him in the 1970s.

At 29, Arribart had been around the block and could see that Wenger was different. Yes, he exhibited the dour Alsatian traits – perfectionism, professionalism. Yes, he was strict, demanding, unswerving. As he would be wherever he went, he was always first to Forêt-de-Haye, the training ground 10 kilometres outside the city, and the last to leave. But in other ways he was experimental, radical, a risk-taker. 'He was one of the first coaches with whom I did different things,' says Arribart. 'To keep players interested he tried to make sure there was a lot of variety in his training sessions. He made us understand why we were doing things, understand our responsibilities on the pitch.'

'I was quite surprised by the things he did,' says Platini. Such as? 'He played a lot. He had a lot of six-a-side, seven-a-side. I never heard people grumble about his coaching. He was very popular. That's rare. He was a natural leader. He knew when to use silence, when to raise his voice.'

Collectors of arcane footballing facts may wish to know that it was at Nancy's training ground in the early 1970s that those wooden dummy walls were first used for free-kick practice. It was also the first club in France to create a *centre de formation*.

Wenger carried on the spirit of innovation. Now that he was his own boss, he seized the chance to implement ideas synthesised from years and years of ceaseless football chat in bars and cafés and training-ground canteens. It wasn't the best squad in France, but he would give it the best chance of succeeding. His first move was to take the team away on a summer training camp. Guillou had done this the year before with Cannes, but only into the hills behind Nice. Never one for half-measures, Wenger identified Val Thorens, an Alpine ski resort, as possessing the highest-altitude football pitch in France. For the next three years, he took the squad back there at the start of July. 'Thanks to him,' says Platini, 'we always had very good starts to the season.'

In came a dietician, spouting unfamiliar nostrums about not snacking between meals, banning energy-sapping puddings, maximising intake of raw or lightly boiled vegetables. When the players sat down to eat in the canteen, they suddenly discovered there was no bread on the table to pick at, and certainly no butter. 'He didn't want the boys to eat before the meal,' says Platini. 'He was severe about it.'

'It was new to us,' says Arribart. Again, attention to diet was something that had been introduced at Cannes by Guillou. A doctor came in and lectured the players on what they should be eating, and what they shouldn't. Even their wives were summoned for briefings, because they were the ones doing the cooking at home. The doctor wrote up a small handbook and distributed it to the squad and the squad's spouses.

It's almost as if Wenger treated Nancy as a private footballing laboratory. One of the great things he would achieve at Arsenal was to acquire a set of apparently ill-fitting jigsaw pieces and find a place for them in a bigger picture. He'd convert Emmanuel Petit from the national team's third-choice left back into its first-choice central midfielder, one who'd score for France in the World Cup final. Like a chess grandmaster he would move Thierry Henry in from the wing, and the cold, and make him into one of the most potent strikers in the world. It happened first at Nancy. When he signed the 20-year-old Eric Bertrand, he was a free-scoring striker from the lower divisions. By the time Wenger left three seasons later, he had refashioned Bertrand into a fullback. In 1986 a left winger called Eric di Meco arrived on loan from Olympique Marseille. Getting only one goal out of him all season, Wenger tried him out at wing back, where he later played for France (twice captaining them) and for Marseille in two European Cup finals.

'Arsène was able to see how the abilities of young players would develop,' says Arribart. 'He understood that a player can play in different positions, depending on his age, his physical build, and his development. That's instinct. You can supplement it by observation, but it's something that you have at the start.' It helped, of course, that Wenger had switched positions himself, from midfield to sweeper.

All this makes him sound like a rather arid theoretician, and that is how he would initially appear to those who watched him on the touchline in England, resolutely opting not to tear out his neatly tamed hair at every reverse, nor punch holes in the air at every goal. Even in the bitterest defeats, he presents to the media a mask that, if not quite impassive, betrays only a hint of an emotional turmoil that may or may not smoulder beneath the surface.

At Nancy there was no mask. When he was angry, it showed. No one at Strasbourg or Cannes ever remembers him shouting as a reserve team coach, but assuming the sole responsibility proved more of a burden.

'At the start of his career he reacted more and he showed emotions more,' says Arribart. 'He has learnt to control his reactions. He has learnt that it's no use throwing tantrums, except for now and then. The rarer a rage is, the stronger, and the more of an impact it has on the players. He understands that anger is not a good way to get a message across to a player. But in the beginning he felt things very personally. He once stopped the team bus to vomit after a game in Lens. 3-0 was something that turned his stomach. He's learnt to control himself. When you're under control you get your message across better.'

Wenger's horror of defeat was not something he had to deal with too much in that first season. Nancy fought their way to a comfortable 12th position. 'Back then the good players stayed in France so there were good players everywhere,' says Platini. 'So we had a good team. We've known better times. When Michel was here we finished fourth. But 12th was very good.'

But in the close season it was impossible to keep the team together. A striker, Robert Jacques, boarded the gravy train to Paris Saint Germain, while the club's most popular and creative player, a Uruguayan midfielder called Ruben Umpierrez, was sold to another Parisian club, Matra Racing. The goalkeeper Bruno Martini, who was good enough to go on to play for France 31 times, went back to Auxerre after a two-year loan period. They got another keeper back from Auxerre called Didier Loiseau, but he injured his shoulder on his debut and was out for six months. A third keeper, between clubs, dashed up from Toulouse and got the job for the rest of the season.

Another player, Denis Hindelang, arrived from the lower division with a debilitating disease of the blood, from which he recovered only to be summoned for six months' military service. He played his first game a year after signing. However much Wenger believed in preparation, he had no choice but to fly by the seat of his pants. For the first time Wenger took the opportunity to look for cheaper talent abroad. He beat off other clubs to sign Adriano Fegic, a Slovenian who had played for Yugoslavia. He wasn't entirely suited to Wenger's Germanic penchant for defenders who could attack and attackers who could defend. Fegic was used to playing in a team built around him. Wenger had to order him to pull his weight in midfield. By the next summer he was gone.

1985-6 was not a success. The average gate went up slightly, but the team went down, if not quite all the way down. Disaster was averted after the last day of the season proper, when Nancy, who finished the season in 17th place, were forced into a play-off with Wenger's old employer, FC Mulhouse, who were runners-up in the second division. So for the second time Wenger found himself involved in a play-off between Mulhouse and Nancy.

On this occasion, 11 years on, the prize was a place in the first division, rather than avoiding relegation to the third. Wenger was on the winning side again. The game was played over two legs: Nancy cantered to a 3-0 victory at home, and then nearly tossed it all away by losing 2-0 in the return. Still, it guaranteed survival, at least for another year.

By now Wenger was thoroughly settled into a routine at Nancy. After every home game he went with the directors to dinner in a local Italian restaurant, a habit he would continue at Arsenal. He lunched once a week at the house of the Platinis near Forêt-de-Haye, where his host claims that they didn't just talk about football. 'He was interested in a lot of things. Politics, life.' (At Strasbourg University Wenger had a lot of friends who were communists. He was always instinctively to the right of centre, and is now cautiously pro-Euro.)

But then Platini adds, 'I don't think he had another life. It was football, football.' As usual, Wenger's own home – he lived in an apartment in the centre of town – was not for entertaining others, or even for others to enter. It was for sleeping, and watching videos of matches. 'I never went to his place,' says Platini. 'Never.' He doesn't remember Wenger having a girlfriend. It was only when he got to Arsenal that a private life – he was 48 when his only child was born – started to eat into his football-oriented schedule. 'For a long time he was single,' says Arribart. 'He's obsessed with football and is constantly looking for ways to improve. He watches a lot of matches. But he has had to change his ways a bit because he has a family, which he never had before. I think he's found a balance: 30 per cent family and 70 per cent football.'

After the second season, there was the now standard exodus from Nancy, starting with Jean-Luc Arribart. Bruno Germain, another industrious midfielder, moved on to bigger things: five years later, like Eric Di Meco, he'd play for Marseille in the European Cup Final. In mid-season, Paris Saint-Germain made their traditional swoop, this time for long-serving, low-scoring 'water-carrier', Eric Martin.

'Sadly, as we didn't have any money, the president sold him,' says Platini. 'He was a fighter, always on the ball, the ideal midfielder. He left an enormous hole. So did Germain.' With Fejic also pushing off, that was almost an entire midfield. With even less money to play with, Wenger's purchases took on a slightly desperate air. In came Philippe Piette, a midfielder who when he arrived at 28 had already played for six clubs. With mixed success Platini sourced a couple of Hungarians who had just played in the World Cup in Mexico. Antal Nagy was the sweeper for the national side. Peter Hannich had scored a lot of goals from midfield in Hungary. He didn't score a single one for Nancy. 'Nagy turned out well,' says Platini. 'Hannich didn't.' There was another farce with the accident-prone goalkeeper Loiseau, who finally made it into the side a year on, only for serious injury to end his season after a few games.

Rousselot says he spent more money that final year than he had in Wenger's two previous seasons. But almost throughout 1986-7, it seems to have been accepted that Nancy were doomed. 'When we went down, we went down,' says Platini. 'Contracts ended, people left, and everyone we wanted to get was too expensive. The president didn't want to buy them. So it was logical that we were relegated. We were completely out of the running.'

It was the only time in over three decades in football that Wenger has had personal experience of the drop. But his behaviour throughout the season was relaxed – eerily so, it might have seemed to the players. If he was suffering from stress, 'he never showed it,' says Platini. This was not unconnected with the fact that he knew his own future was secure. 'When a club goes down it's often the fault of coach. He's the first to be thrown out. As Arsène knew he was leaving, perhaps he was a bit laid back.'

However badly Nancy had done in the league, Wenger had been noticed. The same summer that he won the play-off, he was approached by AS Monaco. He wanted to leave, but there was a year remaining on his contract. Wenger is always painted as someone who honours his contracts. In fact he was all for jumping ship, just as he later did in Japan before his second year was up.

'He wanted to leave for Monaco,' says Rousselot. 'He asked to be freed from the last year of his contract. I refused because first of all I valued him as a coach and it would be difficult to replace him. Also I believed that if Monaco were asking us to release someone who was under contract, all they needed to do was make an offer to compensate the club that was letting its coach go. But at the time that wasn't the done thing. I asked them to buy out his contract and they refused.'

This upshot was not to Wenger's liking. Although Monaco wanted Wenger, they didn't want him quite enough to pay off Nancy. They were quite happy to wait until he was available. According to Rousselot, Wenger 'wasn't too happy about it. It was a body-blow. He regretted that we weren't going to free him, but he's a gentleman. He had a contract and he respected it.' He didn't have much choice.

The inevitable was staved off. Between them, the president, the director of football and the coach kept Monaco's approach a secret. None of the players knew, and certainly not the press. As for Wenger, even as the side he was coaching slipped inexorably down-wards, he knew that he would soon be heading in the other direction, with the result that his attention was not entirely on Nancy's survival in that final season.

A hint of evidence for this is perhaps to be found in his last significant signing. In mid-season Wenger and Platini flew to Scotland to take a look at a Dundee FC centre forward called Ray Stephen. This was Wenger's first active contact with British football. Stephen, pre-dictably good with his head, duly scored twice on his debut, and was seen as a burly cure-all for Nancy's problems in front of goal. He was a '*bâton*', according to Platini – a stick with which to beat French defences. Wenger may also have seen him as an experiment. In Stephen, he was dipping his toe in the water to observe how well a big striker would cope in the Championnat. A bit like Hannich, he wasn't quite up to it. 'We thought for a moment that he'd be our saviour,' says

Rousselot. 'For one or two games he put himself about a bit. He was a good player, but no more than that. He couldn't stop the haemorrhaging.'

At the same time as Ray Stephen was failing to rescue Nancy, Wenger was fantasising about future acquisitions. Only a few months later he would be in a rather better position to pick and choose, and he'd be able to sign a classic British centre forward not from a Scottish backwater but from AC Milan. As well as Mark Hateley, he'd also make another purchase – of perhaps the best British footballer of the age. Satisfyingly, Glenn Hoddle was whipped from under the noses of the club to whom Wenger had lost several of their best players: Paris Saint Germain, coached by Gérard Houllier.

CHAMPION

'When I was 22, a friend told me that she'd been to see a clairvoyant who on learning my astrological sign had declared, "He'll never earn any money." Maybe she meant that I wasn't interested in money. If I've earned money in my life, it's really been an accident. I'm passionate about doing something that just happens to be lucrative... I sometimes say to footballers' agents, "The difference between you and me is that if tomorrow there were no more money in football I'd still be here, but not you."'

Arsène Wenger

AS Monaco play their home games at the Stade Louis II. It is a stadium named after a prince and, in Prince Rainier and Prince Albert, it's fit for a couple of them too. From the outside, though, it doesn't look that way. You could walk right past it and never know it's a stadium at all. Fans visiting from abroad here must wonder if they've come to the right address. How can anyone play football in what is, to all intents and purposes, a block of flats?

It is a vast squat building, hemmed in among other smaller but similar structures. Caught between rock and sea, there is added value in every one of Monaco's 1,950 square metres. When it was built in 1985, the Stade Louis II was thus obliged to wear a number of hats. Dug into the basement is a complex comprising a swimming-pool and a sports hall. Above that there's a four-floor car park with 14,000 spaces. The football ground is, in effect, on the sixth floor. Perhaps ground is the wrong word. It's more as if stadium has landed from outer space in an area of prime real estate. To complete the surreal disguise, there is a cladding of apartments and offices around the exterior of the building. It's a very very long way from Duttlenheim.

Some of those offices are occupied by AS Monaco – some, but not many. There is a cramped reception on the second floor, plus three poky offices – one for the director of football, another shared by the assistant coaches, and a third for first-team coach (name on the door at time of visit: Didier Deschamps). Upstairs there are a few more offices, including one for Richard Conte, the man who in 1983 offered Arsène Wenger a job at Cannes and found him an apartment, but went on to work here as director of public relations. Up another floor and we're through the team bathroom, the odd-shaped home changing room, past the open door to the kit room, festooned in red and white synthetic fabrics. Mount one more staircase and we're walking out onto the pitch.

My guide is Jean-Luc Ettori. To give Ettori a co-ordinate, he was the French keeper when in the opening group game of the 1982 World Cup Bryan Robson scored the fastest goal in the competition's history.

England were later eliminated when Kevin Keegan missed a famous sitter against Spain. Ettori was still there for the semi-final and the notorious body-check by German goalkeeper Harald Schumacher on Patrick Battiston, which not only failed to elicit a criminal charge, it didn't even earn a booking. Ettori was unable to prevent West Germany from winning the penalty shoot-out.

Ettori's family comes from Corsica, and he has the craggy appearance of an island farmer, with a magnificent broken nose as the centrepiece. You wouldn't think this playpen for the tuxedoed super-rich would be his sort of place at all, but he came to Monaco aged 20 in 1975 and retired as a player here 18 years and 602 games later. Arsène Wenger was lucky in the leaders he inherited. At Nagoya Grampus Eight he would have Dragan Stojkovic, the best player to emerge from Yugoslavia in decades. At Arsenal there'd be Tony Adams. At Monaco, he had Ettori. When Wenger was sacked after seven years, it was Ettori who succeeded him. He went on to become the goalkeeping coach.

As Wenger's appointment was kept a secret until the end of his contract, the freshest entry on the newcomer's CV was an ignominious one: led Nancy down into the Second Division. Fans were entitled to ask questions. Not that there were many fans to ask questions, of course. The entire population of Monaco could fit into Highbury and still make generous provision for away supporters. Wenger was about to swap a small fan-base for a smaller one.

Ettori stands behind one of the goals. He is

surprisingly short for a goalkeeper. It is a warm winter Mediterranean day. The pitch is slightly threadbare. The empty stands seem remote. They are low, and solid, and painted in a dull terracotta. It is a stately setting and, with the imperious rockface of the Côte d'Azur up above, somehow unhomely. The classically curving *tribunes* behind each goal seem miles away. 'It holds 18,500,' says Ettori. And how many fans usually come? Gallically, he shrugs. '5,000? When Marseille come they outnumber our fans. It's like a home game for them.' But then the dice were always loaded in favour of Marseille. Wenger would have to get used to that.

A year earlier, Arsène Wenger had not been AS Monaco's first choice – not with a mid-table finish and a relegation play-off to his name. The person the club went to before him was an old patron of his, Gilbert Gress, who in winning the Championnat with Racing Club de Strasbourg in 1979 had used Wenger as a stand-in sweeper in a game against Monaco. After a stint at FC Bruges, Gress had fetched up at Neuchâtel Xamax in Switzerland, where he was winning titles and thriving in European competition. 'I had a great team,' says Gress. 'We got to the quarter-finals of the UEFA Cup twice. We beat Bayern Munich at home 2-1, then lost in the last two minutes of the away leg. So I was happy, and I stayed.' Gress, it seems, was content to turn down the big clubs, just like Paul Frantz, who once rejected AC Milan. Clearly ambition was one thing Wenger didn't learn at the feet of the older men whose company he so favoured. In this one vital area, he was self-taught.

Two people contacted Gress. The first was Henri Biancheri, a former player who now ran AS Monaco on a day-to-day basis as the director of football. The second was the president, Jean-Louis Campora, a doctor of medicine who had once held ministerial office. Gress's refusal gave them a licence to be bold, and they now turned their attention to luring his polar opposite – a studious greenhorn with a growing reputation but nothing, as yet, on his mantelpiece. It was Conte who gave them the idea.

'I had a friendly relationship with the president,' he says. 'When I heard that he was after a coach, I said I thought the man he was looking for was now at Nancy.' Of course it was the same old story for Wenger. 'I realised that no one knew him here.'

This isn't quite true. Biancheri had met him in the early 80s via the Variété Football Club, and had heard of him before then because he worked for Adidas, whose French base is close to Strasbourg. But he knew that Conte knew him much better. 'In a friendly way I got the two of them talking,' says Conte. 'The President didn't know Arsène, Arsène didn't know anyone at Monaco, and so I introduced them. It was confidential. Arsène was under contract at Nancy. They didn't have a lot of money and were much more likely to go down than to stay up.'

It is extremely rare in football for a coach to know what job he will be doing much before he is doing it. It's a measure of how much Wenger was wanted by his clubs that this has happened to him twice in his career: initially when he spent a whole year at Nancy knowing he was bound for Monaco; later when at Nagoya

Grampus Eight he knew he would be going to Arsenal. In each case he took the opportunity to do some preliminary shopping. Long before his appointment was officially confirmed at Arsenal, the cat was more or less let out of the bag when a North London club which had never previously employed any French players suddenly signed two: Rémi Garde and Patrick Vieira.

Something similar happened at Monaco. Wenger finally became a free agent in May 1987. But he had actually been quietly communicating with Biancheri all that year. 'I met him four or five months before the end of the season,' says Biancheri. 'I dealt with the recruitment of players he wanted to get.' Even as Nancy were forced to sell one of their stars, Eric Martin, Monaco under guidance from Nancy's incumbent coach prepared to go into full buying mode.

Wenger's first two signings when he went to England were French. His first two signings at Monaco were English. Mark Hateley still has no idea who at Monaco actually made the move for him. 'I'm not sure whether Arsène bought me or not,' he says. 'We both more or less arrived on the same day. I don't know if he already was doing his deal and knew I was coming or he wanted me to come.' In fact Wenger had a very specific idea of who he wanted to buy. 'Hateley and Hoddle: those were his two choices,' says Biancheri.

But as Wenger was stuck at Nancy, it was impossible for him to do his own scouting. Biancheri went to watch Hateley two or three times playing for Milan and reported back to Wenger. Hateley was only 21 when he went to Italy, and in his first year had scored a towering header to win the derby against Internazionale. But he had not had a particularly distinguished World Cup in Mexico in 1986, when he was dropped after two bad results. With Gary Lineker's goals, England immediately started winning, until they came up against Diego Maradona's hand of God.

Wenger kept his eyes peeled on the international market and sensed an opening. Italian clubs were allowed to field only three foreigners, and AC Milan were in the process of buying up the best players in Holland, who would win the European Championship the following year: Ruud Gullit, Marco Van Basten and Frank Rijkaard. In Milan, Hateley was not wanted on voyage. 'We knew that there was the possiblity of a transfer,' says Biancheri.

Signing Glenn Hoddle required greater sleight of hand. The Tottenham chairman Irving Scholar kept a boat in Monaco and knew Campora. 'We knew from him that they were going to give Hoddle a free transfer for his services,' says Biancheri. 'As soon as I heard, I talked to Arsène.' Wenger, understandably, was keen. It was February. Nancy continued to toil, and Peter Hannich, his midfield purchase from Hungary, had flopped. Here was his chance to sign a number 10 of whom Michel Platini would say, 'If he'd been French he'd have won 100 caps.' Wenger dispatched Biancheri to watch England play against Spain in Madrid. It was the first time the countries had met since Keegan missed his sitter in the World Cup five years earlier. Lineker scored four. If Wenger had been able to go, he would have seen Tony Adams win his first cap. Unfortunately, Paris Saint Germain were also interested, and by the summer Hoddle was on his way to the capital to sign for a team coached by Gérard Houllier. At the last minute Monaco intervened, and Hoddle flew on down to the Côte d'Azur. On Wenger's instruction they also bought Battiston, a central defender with 50 caps to his name but out of contract at Bordeaux. He also secured Luc Sonor, a midfielder, from Metz, who was promptly picked for France. 'We built a team for his arrival,' says Biancheri.

Biancheri is a proper man of the south, hunched and bullet-shaped and demonstrative. He comes in the Latin livery of a tight black T-shirt, a gold necklace and, even in winter, a deep tan set off by a halo of cropped white hair. He retired from playing in 1965 after a career spent largely at Monaco, with whom he won two Championnats, two Coupes de France and two international caps.

For 20 years he was director of Adidas in the south of France, until Campora and Prince Rainier asked him to return. When Wenger came, Biancheri had only been in the job a year, and when we meet it still looks as if he's only just moved into his small box of an office. His desk is more or less empty. A black and white photo of the Monaco team from the early 60s stands propped against the wall. It may have been there for years.

Biancheri found a club in stasis. A coach had just left and, while they awaited Wenger, 65-year-old Stefan Kovacs filled in. His was quite a pair of shoes to step into. Kovacs had coached Steaua Bucharest,

Romania, France and, most impressively, the great Ajax side which won three European Cups in the early 70s. The appointment of a young, untried successor was part of a long-term business plan. Capitalising on Wenger's background in youth development, the idea was to rebuild, methodically, carefully, patiently, to reconstruct the club from the bottom up and produce another championship-winning side within a couple of years. In the end it didn't quite happen that way.

Wenger inherited a good team whose two stars were defenders – Ettori in goal, and France's most capped player, Manuel Amoros, at full back. With the surgical insertion of his two Englishmen, it became a team in Wenger's own image, reconfigured to maximise these new talents. Henceforth, the majority of the play was to be channelled through Hoddle. Next to him in midfield was a classic French water-carrier called Claude Puel, who joined the club a year or two after Ettori. 'Puel wasn't a great player with the ball but he was indispensable,' says Ettori. His job was to win the ball and give it to Hoddle.

'As soon as you had a problem with the ball, you gave it to Glenn,' says Puel. 'In England, where it was the era of the long ball, he had been a bit misunderstood. In France the game was more suited to him and he had three extraordinary years at Monaco. It was him who organised everything, who made all the difference.'

With the ball at his feet, Hoddle could look up and consider his options. He had a wing back in Amoros shunting up and down the flank, plus a ferociously quick and fitfully skilful Youssouf Fofana, who had been brought to Cannes from the Ivory Coast by Jean-Marc Guillou. Or he could always pitch the ball onto Hateley's head.

'We would get the ball forward quickly to Glenn,' remembers Hateley. 'We didn't want him to come out the centre circle or into his own half. He would either find me or the wide players and then the ball would be played into me and he would support me or I would take the chance. We terrorised everybody we played against.' Hateley has never been a wildly free-scoring forward, but he was able to scare French defences far more than he ever scared Italian ones.

'He was a typical English striker,' says Ettori: 'A force of nature, an animal, afraid of nothing. French defences weren't used to someone so combative, so tough. When you think of a tough player you think of a defender. But he was tough – tough on others, tough on himself. He pulled us all along with his energy. And he had an English spirit: always winning. In France you win at home and try not to lose away. He and Glenn wanted to win all the time.'

By the end of the season, Hateley finished second highest goalscorer behind Jean-Pierre Papin of Marseille. But Monaco finished in front of Marseille. Way ahead of schedule, they won the title.

How much did Wenger have to do with all of this? Certainly the players weren't expecting much from him. 'The choice surprised us a little bit as players,' says Ettori. 'He came from a club that had been relegated. But after a fortnight we understood why he was there, that he was the man we needed.' Before everything else, Wenger was lucky. The team had just been through a lean patch. The club had won the title in 1978, the year before Strasbourg, and again in 1982. They also reached the final of the Coupe de France in 1980 and 1985. It was the greatest period in the club's history. And then suddenly, for two seasons, things stagnated.

'When he arrived there was a turning point,' says Puel. 'It's always easier when you arrive at a club that's had an average season to get things going again because players are much more receptive. They want to progress. He boosted players who had had a difficult season.'

The players, in other words, were waiting for someone to take charge, to tell them what to do, 'to get into their heads,' says Ettori, 'that no result was possible without sacrifice. But he did it gently. Arsène had such confidence in himself that you had confidence in yourself.' When the squad returned for pre-season training in Switzerland, he talked to each player individually. Ettori still remembers the conversation 16 years on. 'The year before I didn't have a great season. When Arsène was at Cannes, he came to games at Monaco a lot. He said, "I want to see the Ettori that I used to see all the time."'

His confidence expressed itself in the certainty of his own beliefs. The tactics, as at Arsenal, were for the players to impose themselves collectively on their opponents. 'He wasn't going to adapt himself to the opposition. He wasn't going to instruct a player to stop the other team.' At Nancy he had played the classic 4-4-2, and he deployed the same formation here. He knew the system inside out, and in 20 years he has never really strayed from it. He made the players fit the system, but he made sure they were the best players.

This is where Wenger's interest in group psychology had its first real road-test. If the players needed a leader on the touchline, they also needed a leader on the pitch. Wenger was astute enough to understand that the existing players had no problem with the idea of serving a team built around one incoming player, so long as that player was good enough. In Hoddle, who never learnt much French, he found someone who was as free from self-doubt as a player as Wenger was as a coach. Ettori, who was club captain, shakes his head in wonderment at the memory of Hoddle. 'For us Glenn was *le bon dieu* – he was a god. There's nothing else to say. He was the star but he didn't have the caprices of a star. For me, the time he was in France, he was the best player in the world.'

Though only 37 when he arrived at Monaco, Wenger exerted a similar hold over his players. He energised them with his conviction, and with his attention to detail. In his methodical Alsatian way, he set about turning the club upside down. It started at the training ground, La Turbie, ten kilometres outside Monaco up in the hills. Before his arrival, the club was not especially professional in its approach to coaching. No sooner had he arrived than he insisted that everything be done his way. Suddenly the teams through all the levels were required to play the same system. It was 4-4-2 and no deviation. Training sessions were extremely hard work – short and intense and done to the stopwatch.

'We worked our socks off on the training ground,' says Hateley. 'We would do things in set times. Even if you're halfway through a routine it stops and it goes on to the next. I think we understood what it was for. A lot of the stuff is a variation on a theme. It's the same exercise disguised in a different procedure: to keep your mind sharp, to make sure that you're thinking all the time. You're working the areas that you need to work: your mind, your body, your feet, quick thinking.'

They began with a long warm-up and ended with thorough stretches, run by the physios but with Wenger overseeing. Enzo Scifo, the Belgian playmaker signed from Torino as a successor to Hoddle, remembers his training sessions as 'quite explosive and shorter compared with other coaches I've had. They are carefully designed to be effective and very enjoyable for the players. He puts a lot of stress on the technical side. His sessions have a lot of technical moves, and repeated phases of play.' Why do these players use the present tense? It's as if Wenger's coaching methods are still with them.

To all players he remained enigmatic, unknowable. He'd talk with them during training, ensure that they were happy at home. But he never allowed his charges to get close. 'You could always go to see him and discuss things,' says Puel, 'but he had a certain distance with the players. In his manner, in his speech, he had a natural authority. He didn't need to force it.' Ettori remembers 'this rather austere attitude. You respected him. For us he was the boss. Even if he joked with us, there was always this barrier between us and him.'

Wenger made a sort of physical audit of each player. He brought in specialists – physios, a sprint expert, a weight expert, a doctor – to hone the players into thoroughbreds. He was messianic about his beliefs concerning eating and drinking. It's not that the players hadn't heard any of this stuff before. 'We'd more or less followed it for years,' says Jean Petit, whom Wenger inherited as his assistant coach. 'But Arsène made people understand that to get the best out of yourself, you had to train, to rest and to eat well.' And travel well. Haphazard arrangements for getting to away games were done away with. The club chartered planes and flew to the north of France. Ettori calls it Wenger's 'invisible coaching'.

It was a benevolent autocracy, enforced by an iron fist in a velvet glove. He insisted on punctuality, and laid down the law about who could come into the dressing-room before games. 'Arsène said, "OK, in the dressing-room there's me, my assistant, the physio and the president. Stop,"' says Petit. 'That's not easy. Here of all places. He had the power to say no.' Why? 'Because he's Arsène Wenger. The coaches who came after didn't have Arsène's charisma.' The force of his charisma enabled him to stop short of just barking out orders. 'He explained things to the players,' says Petit. 'It wasn't a case of "if you do this" or "if you don't do that". He wasn't even saying anything that big. But he used *le mot juste*. When he told you something, you believed. He was a bit like a pastor.' 'He had this certainty which reassured everyone,' says Ettori, 'even if he wasn't sure himself if it was the right thing to be doing.'

Wenger was not all revolutionary at Monaco, just as he wouldn't be at Arsenal, where he retained the *ancien régime*'s praetorian rearguard, the back four trained by George Graham. He was also an evolutionary. Far from fear for his livelihood, Jean Petit was instantly given to understand that his job as assistant coach was safe.

Nor were any of the coaching techniques he brought in remotely new, at least not to Hateley, whose recent experience at Milanello, the AC Milan training facility, Wenger was keen to tap. Using his English, he debriefed his young acquisition about training schedules, warm-up techniques and stretch routines used in Milan. 'He was the first manager that I know that came and asked questions of players,' says Hateley. 'Arsène didn't play at a high level and if you've got players that have played at the highest level, it's foolish not to ask advice. He was only young in the early stages of his managerial career. He was very raw.'

Not content with Hateley's testimony, he occasionally got in the car and went to Milanello to look for himself. At the same time, coaches started to turn up on his doorstep: Philippe Troussier, Michel Platini and his successor as coach of the national team, Gérard Houllier. La Turbie, under Wenger's wing, became a sort of Socratic footballing academy. He was in a perpetual dialogue with Petit that would go on for hours after each morning session. Biancheri would join in. So would the youth and reserve team coach.

'It never stopped,' says Biancheri. 'He's the kind of person who can talk about football for ten hours without stopping. And it's a pleasure. You don't notice the time passing.' Petit confirms that this is no exaggeration, but that they did manage to slip in other topics. 'Life. Women.'

This is how much interest Wenger took in the rest of his life: when he first moved down to Cannes, his friend Richard Conte found him an apartment in the same block in Villefranche-sur-Mer; he found him another when he came back down to Monaco. 'He was meant to stay for three months and then look for something else,' says Conte. 'He stayed for seven years.' He more or less lived at La Turbie.

In the team hotel on Friday nights, the coaching staff would send the players to bed and stay down in the restaurant talking for an hour or more. Wenger was nervous before home games. 'He came from a small club,' says Petit, 'to a big club where results were expected.' He also found the lack of atmosphere difficult. It's not as if he knew much about big crowds, but to play in front of small crowds in such a dramatic stadium deprived the players of motivation. He had to supply his own.

At Arsenal he has lost his temper only a handful of times. At Monaco, for all his maniacal self-control, it happened rather more often. 'He had a ferocious temper,' recalls Hateley. This usually manifested itself at half-time. 'If things weren't going right the veins in his neck would just pop out and he'd throw it right into you. He was very stubborn. He had a vision and it was to be done his way. He had the players to do what we needed to do. If he asked a player to do something which he knew he could do he would lash them in front of everybody and wouldn't play him.'

Scifo remembers a training session that hadn't gone well. 'Nothing was going right. The players gave the impression that they weren't trying, and they could feel Arsène was getting ready to explode. He sent all the players to the changing room and he wanted to see the whole team in there, and he was really angry. We'd never seen him like that. It really astonished most of the team because we weren't used to it. For me it was the first time I'd seen Arsène angry. He was very hard on certain players. He's the type of person who doesn't get any joy out of getting angry. You want to work with him because he has this human side that you really appreciated. He never deceives you. He's very honest in everything he does. When he reproaches you for something you know he's right. There's no argument. You can never say he's not telling the truth.'

If occasionally he erupted at half-time, before the game he was calm. His routine was always the same. The morning of the game the squad would visit the stadium and go over various things on the pitch. Then there was a meeting in which Wenger talked about the opposition for 45 minutes to an hour: who to pick up, who to watch, how they played. Wenger had a drawing board with diagrams. Players would ask questions. Occasionally, he'd talk in English if Hateley or, more particularly, Hoddle hadn't understood. Then, for home games, they'd repair to the Beach Plaza for a pre-match meal at about midday, after which the squad would sleep or rest all afternoon. There was another meeting at five in the hotel, for about an hour, in which the opposition was not mentioned once.

'You've already learnt what they were going to do and you've slept on that,' says Hateley. 'Subconsciously you've gone to bed thinking about the opposition, which is psychologically very good. The last thing that we would talk about for an hour would be us and nothing else so that the thing you had in your mind when you were going onto that pitch was what you were going to do.'

For all his dogmatism, his belief in punctuality and obedience to the goals of the group, Wenger gave his players their freedom. The hard work, the organisation, the unswerving strictness – they were all calculated to ensure that nothing went wrong. But inspiration was down to the individual, and the system helped.

'He likes you to express yourself,' says Scifo. 'That's his asset. He is very insistent about the team keeping its shape. The most important thing is to have a foundation on the pitch. But then he gives a lot of freedom to the players. In the end, he likes football. He doesn't neglect the artistic side. He has married efficiency to spectacle. He picks players who can put on a show.' That's why he bought Hoddle, and then Scifo, and why when Mark Hateley sustained an injury early on in the second season which kept him out for nearly two years, he turned to a young Liberian called George Weah.

That first year it worked: Monaco won the championship. And yet Wenger was never one for overt celebration. Henri Biancheri remembers merely that he was pleased – 'pleased for himself, for the president, and for the princes'. The entire squad was summoned for a reception at the Grimaldi palace, secluded high on the rock that splits Monaco in half. For Wenger, winning the French championship was the culmination of a lifetime's obsession: it was the prize for study, for self-improvement, the pilgrimages to West Germany with Max Hild, for all the time he'd spent in cafés with friends who were far more talented footballers, the long slog of acquiring his badges more slowly than the pros, for all those thousands of hours in front of the videos, for devoting his every waking hour to the game.

The next six years at Monaco would be good, but they would never be quite this good.

EUROPEAN

'Some people found my belief in fair play ridiculous, because in high-level sport the idea of fair play is linked with defeat.'

Arsène Wenger

The goal of every coach on the continent is to win the European Cup. The competition was dreamed up by a Frenchman, but when Arsène Wenger arrived in Monaco it had never been won by a French club. By the time he left, it had.

For a variety of reasons, it was a moment in the history of European football when, briefly, anything seemed possible. Wenger was at the Parc des Princes stadium in Paris in 1975 for the European Cup final when the seat-hurling high jinks of Leeds United hooligans got their club banned from European competition for three years. A decade later, Liverpool fans at the Heysel stadium in Belgium outdid them: the death of 39 people, all but one of them Juventus fans, after a wall collapsed, secured a five-year ban from Europe for all English clubs. As they had monopolised the European Cup for most of those ten years, their absence levelled the playing-field for everyone else.

This was before the creation of the Champions League, the Bosman transfer ruling and the proliferation of satellite television allowed the aristocrats of the game to pull away from the rest. It was also before the fall of the Berlin Wall, so clubs from Eastern Europe still kept their best players. During Wenger's tenure at Monaco, both Steaua Bucharest and Red Star Belgrade got as far as the European Cup final. So did Porto and Benfica of Portugal. It was as good a chance as French football was going to get to challenge the élite from Italy, Spain and Germany.

Wenger had played once in Europe, in Strasbourg's 4-0 drubbing on an ice rink in Duisberg. His first game in Europe as a coach was, appropriately, in Iceland, and in its own way, it proved just as slippery. Monaco lost 1-0 to Valur of Reykjavík, before winning 2-0 at the Stade Louis II. A win over FC Bruges, Gilbert Gress's old club, brought them to the quarter-finals, where they lost at home to Galatasaray, drew away, and were eliminated. It wouldn't be the last time the Turkish club would stand in Wenger's way.

As first efforts go, it wasn't bad. Wenger looked forward to many more assaults on the highest peak in club football. In fact he'd have to wait a further five years to compete again in the European Cup, and even then admission would be by the back door. The unfortunate truth for Wenger is that Monaco is not the French club everyone remembers from that era. Olympique Marseille is.

When Monaco won the championship in 1988, Marseille finished sixth. They then proceeded to win the title five times in a row and twice reach the

European Cup final. Only AC Milan stood in the way of continental supremacy. One of the reasons that they were able to dominate so utterly is that they had home crowds of 30,000, the largest in France by far. It was an incalculable advantage. The advantage was financial, of course – Monaco's royal backing was not enough to match that income week after week. But it was also more intangible. In the end there was no substitute for playing in front of a full house at home. Several of Monaco's players thought so. A year after he won the title, Wenger lost his best defender and France's most capped player, Manuel Amoros, to Marseille. A year on from that, he managed to poach Franck Sauzée, an international midfielder, from his rivals, but he stayed for only one season before returning. Gil Rui Barros, a Portuguese international, arrived from Juventus, but also left for Marseille after two years at Monaco.

And if Wenger was able to sign top players, his rivals simply signed more. A charismatic tycoon and, subsequently, government minister, Bernard Tapie took over the presidency in 1986, and proceeded to cram the club with superstars. The Marseille team-sheets during Wenger's time at Monaco included French internationals such Jean-Pierre Papin, Eric Cantona, Basile Boli, Didier Deschamps, Jocelyn Angloma and Marcel Desailly. Not quite as illustriously, but gallingly for Wenger, Marseille also fielded two players he had nurtured at Nancy: Bruno Germain and Eric di Meco. In their period of ascendancy, Marseille frequently provided more than half the national side.

And then there were the foreigners: over the years, Wenger found himself having to prepare his defences to confront not only Papin, the Championnat's perennial top scorer, but also Enzo Francescoli, Dragan Stojkovic, Alen Boksic, Abedi Pelé, Rudi Völler, Paolo Futre and Chris Waddle, all among the most gifted footballers in the world. Waddle left Tottenham for the south of France partly on the advice of his old team-mate Hoddle. 'If we could have had another foreigner,' says Henri Biancheri, 'we would have had Chris Waddle. But Marseille had more money than us. Bernard Tapie assembled an extraordinary team.'

But Tapie did not just use money to buy the best foreign players France had ever seen. It was by foul means as well as fair that he made it effectively impossible for Wenger to repeat the achievement of his first year. If ever Wenger has cause to detest anyone in football, it is Tapie. 'With Arsène and Tapie,' says Jean Petit, 'it was war to the death.'

All of this was in the future when the squad reassembled in the summer of 1988. The first thing to go wrong coincided with the second: the injury that ended Mark Hateley's career at Monaco occurred in the tie with Galatasaray. A replacement was on hand, if not quite a ready-made one. George Weah was recommended to Wenger by Claude Leroi, a Cameroon-based coach, when he and Biancheri attended the Africa Nations Cup in Morocco in March 1988. Biancheri was sent on a bizarre errand down to Cameroon, where Weah was playing for Yaoundé, to secure his signature. It involved opening his suitcase and distributing thousands of francs to a variety of interested parties. Weah was Wenger's first signing from Africa. He was one of the first to identify the former French colonies as an untapped source. In Luc Sonor and Lilian Thuram, he took on two naturalised Frenchmen born in Guadeloupe. From Senegal he signed Roger Mendy, a formidable *libero* physically in the mould of Desailly.

In 1991, *France Football* adjudged that Monaco had three of the ten best African players in the world. It says much for Wenger's nose that Weah went on to become the first African to win the World and European Player of the Year awards. He dedicated his World Player award to Wenger.

To start with, Weah's talent wasn't always obvious. Hateley, who played with him in the autumn of 1988, remembers a boy with 'an uncanny knack for doing things with the ball, but he couldn't do it regular. Sometimes he couldn't trap a dead rat, honestly. And then sometimes he would pull the ball out of the air, swivel it between his legs, nutmeg two players, dance round the goalkeeper and score a goal. Arsène saw the latter in him.'

Wenger's system required a big presence in attack. Weah, for a few seasons, provided it. 'He was inexperienced,' says Hateley. 'He was a raw raw talent. He had to be well looked after, helped along. But Arsène had that ability to encourage players in a way that they would want to repay what he was actually giving to them.' When Wenger went to Arsenal, Weah was keen to rejoin him there from Milan. But Wenger had his eye on another younger forward he had developed at Monaco: Thierry Henry.

Despite the eccentic manner of his signing, Weah was part of a continuum. Wenger may have had access to transfer funds, but nothing like as much as Marseille. Players like Sonor, Fabrice Poullain, Jérôme Gnako and Marcel Dib won caps when they played under Wenger, but in a piecemeal, walk-on fashion. To stay in touch with Marseille, Wenger had to rely on skills he had been developing for ten years: propagating talent, or locating it cheaply. Needless to say, he did it the Alsatian way. He put the hours in. First-team games were on Saturday night. On Sunday afternoons he'd watch the youth teams – the under 15s, the under 17s. He'd maintain contact with the youth coach Pierre Tournier, made sure he took an interest in all the young players at the *centre de formation*. 'He threw himself into it from start to finish, morning till night,' says Biancheri.

In this Wenger was part of a national tide. It was a period when France twigged before any other country that a future World Cup would be won by developing an élite generation of teenagers.

'He realised that young players were going to count,' says Biancheri. 'You can see that in that period. France advanced hugely in coaching. Thanks to people like Arsène Wenger, we produced players like Petit, Henry.' Emmanuel Petit was fast-tracked by Wenger into the first team squad from the reserves as a way of taking the player's mind off the recent death of his brother. He made his debut at 17, and was a regular by 18. Much later, Thierry Henry also started at 17. Thuram got into the team at 18. It was Thuram who from right back scored the two goals that beat Croatia in the World Cup semi-final in 1998.

According to Tony Adams, one of the reasons why Thuram became such a commanding player was Wenger's patience with him at Monaco. 'It cost him game after game,' says Adams. 'But he kept him on. He didn't have financial backing, and encouraged him and encouraged him. Great for the player, no good for him and the team.' Other young players were imported from elsewhere, notably the 22-year-old Youri Djorkaeff from Strasbourg and, right at the end of Wenger's time in Monaco, the 17-year-old David Trezeguet from Argentina.

Wenger had two related gifts: for noticing young talent and for nurturing it. The nurturing was partly a case of being a benign authoritarian the players wanted to please. On a purely technical level, it also involved maximising a player's talents. Just as he didn't want Hoddle to do anything alien to his nature – break sweat, for example – so a version of that rule applied to each individual.

'He appreciated what every player brought to the game,' says Hateley. 'Where all British coaches fall down is to take too much of the good stuff in a player and try and get him better at what he's not good at.' Henry, whom Wenger spotted at the FFF's national *centre de formation* at Clairefontaine, started out as a centre forward at Monaco under Wenger. It was subsequent coaches who attempted to convert him into a winger. When he returned to Arsenal, Wenger coaxed him back into the middle.

'Thanks to Arsène Wenger he's the best attacker in

the world,' says Biancheri. 'Henry was over-endowed with talent. He was intelligent, and with huge potential. Even when he was with us he was strong, and very fast. It wasn't Wenger who gave him that. But he exploited it.' 'Thierry exploded at Monaco,' says Enzo Scifo. 'He had the ability to react with incredible power. Arsène rated him enormously. He always said that he had big big future and he wasn't wrong. He had huge ability for a young player.'

Weah and Petit were the two young players first introduced by Wenger. After elimination from the European Cup, they finished third behind Marseille in the championship in May 1989. With Monaco freshly deposed as champions, the two clubs met in the final of the Coupe de France. It was the best cup final in years, but Wenger's team lost 4-3. Papin scored his first hat trick in three years at Marseille. Marseille thus won the league and cup double. Monaco's consolation was a place, as losing finalists, in the European Cup Winners' Cup. They duly reached the semi-final, where they lost to Sampdoria, but again finished third in the league. The following season, 1990-91, brought another meeting with Marseille in the final of the Coupe de France. Marseille were demoralised after losing on penalties to Red Star Belgrade in the European Cup final a few days earlier. This time a much less absorbing game produced a late winner for Monaco, scored by new signing Gérald Passi. Apart from the championship in his first season, it was the only trophy that Wenger won with Monaco.

Wenger's tenure at Monaco is usually seen as a golden phase in his career when he acquired a reputation across the continent. In truth it was as much a period of intense frustration. Within two years of arriving at Arsenal, he had personally overseen the construction of the perfect training facility at London Colney, which was modelled on a facility he built in his time in Nagoya. He actually essayed something similar at Monaco. When he arrived at La Turbie, a spectacular retreat high up in the mountains with a sheer drop along one edge, the squad changed in Portakabins. Wenger's idea was to build a training ground fit for champions – incorporating more pitches, a physio room, a small hotel, and proper offices. The plans were all approved. But in Wenger's time it was never built.

It somehow symbolised Wenger's difficulties that he lost the two English talismen of his title-winnng side to injury: Hateley in November 1988, Hoddle exactly two years later. A vague whiff of misfortune and ill omen attached itself to the club. Even now, Jean Petit, who was Wenger's assistant, lists a catalogue of refereeing decisions which may just have gone against them, most notably a penalty awarded to Gianluca Vialli in the first leg of the semi-final against Sampdoria. Did Wenger have his suspicions? 'Inevitably he did,' says Petit, 'because when the whistle goes and you've dominated a match and lost 1-0, because of a penalty...' The end of the sentence hangs unsaid. 'In six years there were several instances of the referee not having a good game.'

The best chance the club had of winning a European trophy was in 1992, when they got to the final of the Cup Winners' Cup. The run, which brought hard-won victories over Roma and Feyernoord, started with Wenger's first competitive visit to Britain (in which Monaco overcame the might of Swansea City). Their opponents in the final were Werder Bremen. Then catastrophe struck. The day before the game a temporary stand collapsed in Bastia where the second-division Corsican side were due to play Marseille in the semi-final of the Coupe de France. Eighteen people died, and 2,300 were injured. The next day the Monaco players were besieged by reporters in Lisbon. Wenger would have led them on a ramble around the city. Instead they walked around the third floor.

'We didn't go out the whole day,' recalls Biancheri. 'It's not an excuse, but in the way they approached the game, in their spirit, they were completely absent. Unarguably we deserved to lose.' Which they did, 2-0. Biancheri remembers that Wenger 'was like everyone else, but he didn't let it show because of the pride in his character. He controls himself.'

It was Weah's last big game for Monaco. That summer he went to Paris Saint Germain, who had made a habit of buying Wenger's best players at Nancy. After the tragedy at Bastia, the Coupe de France was cancelled. Monaco had already reached the final.

That year Monaco finished second in the league to Marseille. They were creeping up on them. And yet Wenger began to suspect foul play. An entire year before it was finally discovered that Marseille had bribed players from an opposing team, he noticed that certain members of his own team appeared to have become suddenly clumsy. They gave away penalties. They handballed accidentally. Games that should have been won were drawn. Games that should have been drawn were lost. Not many games, but enough to alert Wenger and his team that, to use Biancheri's phrase, something 'not very catholic' was afoot. 'At the time it was difficult to prove,' says Biancheri. 'The thing we knew was that Marseille had a very good team. But we all thought, a bit naively, that to become champions of France didn't involve anything other than football.'

Wenger has not talked publicly about this long-term trauma in his life. He never confided in the players, but Claude Puel is sure that 'he would have been very angry not to be able to compete on equal terms'. The man who was closest to him at Monaco gives some sense of how distraught he actually was. Jean Petit, like many of those whom Wenger worked with at Monaco, has devoted his adult life to the club. He arrived in 1969 as a player. In the year Monaco won the title straight after promotion, he briefly played in the French midfield alongside Michel Platini and Jean-Marc Guillou. He is short, grey and rather tubby these days, with a genial face and a thick accent of the south.

Petit was the only other person in the room when Wenger confronted one of the players in his side and lured him into admitting that he had been paid to throw games. The player was from a part of the world where, as Wenger knew from the purchase of Weah, the greasing of palms was a more standard procedure than it is in Alsace.

'We had players who were paid by Marseille,' says Petit. 'Arsène had his suspicions. It's not easy to prove. It was the player who confessed to us. We said, "You know, that day? Something happened." We used nuance. We bluffed a bit. And the player said, "Yes. Something did happen."'

The player undergoing this unminuted cross-examination behind close doors was a defender, and so on the pitch he was the link between Jean-Luc Ettori in goal and Puel in midfield. Both had been at the club since the mid-1970s, and both would go on to be club coach.

'They were two guys who would have given their life for their club,' says Petit. 'Like Adams at Arsenal. When they learnt that the player next to them had betrayed them…' Again, he doesn't finish the sentence.

Wenger acted swiftly and uncompromisingly. 'It was the end of the season. Arsène said he had to be kicked out of the team.' The player, who has never been identified, was immediately sold to a lowly club in the Italian Serie A, who were relegated by the end of the year. But there were two other players still under suspicion whom he was never able to arraign. 'They carried on because they didn't confess,' recalls Petit. 'But they didn't stay long.'

The game Wenger was probably referring to was one in April 1992, towards the end of a very tight championship, in which Monaco lost 3-0 at the Stade Louis II to Marseille. It was three days after they'd qualified for the final of the Cup Winners' Cup by beating Feyernoord. In fact Wenger had his doubts about several games. There was no way of knowing how many results were tainted. For Wenger, with his Alsatian sense of honesty and straightness, even the faintest whiff of foul play was insupportable. In his quiet way, he fumed at both the betrayal, and the sense that the injustice could not be redressed. And while he was able to start putting his own house in order by selling at least one of his traitors, he could not stop Tapie buying up other opponents.

It was only a year later, at the end of 1992-93, that Wenger's worst fears were confirmed when the scandal known as *l'affaire VA-OM* was blown open. It concerned a match between Marseille and Valenciennes on 20 May 1993 in which three players for the Valenciennes team were offered a bribe by a Marseille player, Jean-Jacques Eydelie. Valenciennes went on to lose 1-0. To anyone not personally affected, it was a colourful story. Eydelie telephoned an old team-mate, Christophe Robert, in his hotel room. Two other players were there at the time. One was Jorge Burruchaga, who scored the winning goal for Argentina in the World Cup final in 1986. He subsequently claimed that, after initially accepting the bribe, he chose to play as normal. They were uncovered by the third player, Jacques Glassmann, who told the referee at half-time about the bribery attempt. The press had no inkling of this until after the game, when Glassmann spilled the beans. Many of them had been waiting for this story to blow for years.

'The hype was quite incredible,' says Xavier Rivoire, who was reporting on the game for a local radio station. 'Glassman was there in the middle of this over-excited crowd of reporters. He was saying they had been bribed, people had received money, Robert was one of them, and Burruchaga. It was unbelievable.' The whistle-blower was, with a certain inevitability, from Alsace. Perhaps that would explain why all France decided to shoot the messenger. A few weeks later Rivoire spent some time with Glassmann in Valenciennes's pre-season training camp near Lac Léman.

'He was almost a dead man walking. I interviewed him over a coffee and he drank maybe five espressos in the course of half an hour and smoked about two packs of cigarettes. He was lost, completely lost. Every time he played in France from that moment people whistled him, booed him, insulted him, even though he had told the truth. Even the press did not give him a sympathetic hearing.'

A suitcase containing 250,000 francs was found buried in the garden of Robert's parents-in-law. The new season was already underway by the time an inquiry declared the match a draw. The retroactive loss of two points still left Marseille as clear champions, but their title was withdrawn. Rather than give it to Paris Saint Germain, who finished just ahead of Monaco, it was decided to leave the championship vacant. Although there was eventually a court case, at the end of which Tapie was imprisoned, the damage to Monaco, and in particular to Wenger, could not be undone. If Glassmann was the biggest fall guy of the scandal, next in the queue was Wenger. He'd had silverware whipped from under his nose. No one knows how much, but it's widely assumed that as the various

henchmen of Tapie had been at the club for the duration of their success, the entire run is open to suspicion. 'Arsène said that out of the five titles that
Marseille won,' says Biancheri, 'perhaps two were
stolen from us. We could have had two or more.' 'We
had as strong a team as them,' adds Petit. 'So they
should have won three times and us twice, or the other
way round.'

After two years at Arsenal, Wenger would astonish
English football by offering to replay an FA Cup tie
against Sheffield United after his own team stole what
he conceded was an unsporting victory. Nwankwo
Kanu raced onto a throw-in from his own team-mate
that was intended to return possession to the opposition after an injury, and scored. Kanu was making his
Arsenal debut, and was not familiar with the conven-
tion. The same man who would act so generously in
this instance had to suffer in silence as his rivals
cheated in France in the early 1990s. According to
Puel, Wenger 'never accepted defeat too easily. He
always took time to recover.' But this was a bigger
defeat, a seismically unjust one in which the opposition were playing by different rules. It is the one defeat
from which he has never quite recovered. Another of
his confidants was Jean-Marc Guillou, who had
brought him down to the Côte d'Azur in the first
place to run the *centre de formation* at Cannes.

'He has always been very frustrated at being beat-
en, in his opinion, in an irregular manner,' says
Guillou. 'There's nothing more unpleasant for a
sportsman than to be beaten by someone who cheats.
He's such a winner that when he loses when he doesn't

deserve to, it's always going to hurt. Every time I've talked about it with him, I sense that the wound hasn't healed. It was a real body blow. Arsène will never forgive the people who did it.'

UEFA was more stringent than internal French justice. Six days after the Valenciennes game, Marseille won the inaugural Champions League in Munich, beating Milan by Boli's solitary goal. Eydelie was one of the unused substitutes who held the famous trophy aloft. Although no longer technically French champions, they still qualified for next year's competition as holders. But UEFA disqualified them.

Wenger, as a result, had a kind of redress after all. After Paris Saint Germain turned it down, Monaco took Marseille's place in the Champions League in 1993-94. They beat AEK Athens and Steaua Bucharest, and went into a group from which the two leaders qualified for the semi-final. Monaco finished second behind Barcelona, who beat them twice, although they had the satisfaction of twice defeating Galatasaray, their conquerors the previous time Wenger had led Monaco into the competition. The semi-final found them drawn against AC Milan, the club that had offloaded Hateley before embarking on their remarkable domination of Europe, the club whose training ground Wenger had visited to gather knowledge about coaching. Having won their group, Milan had home advantage for the single tie. The two stars of Wenger's side were Enzo Scifo and Jürgen Klinsmann, who was bought from Internazionale to replace Weah. Milan neutralised the threat of Klinsmann, whom they knew well from his two seasons at Internazionale, by kicking lumps out of him. 'They were too strong for us,' recalls Ettori. Monaco lost 3-0. It was more or less Ettori's last big game for Monaco. Wenger didn't have much time left either.

Tapie may have gone down, but in a sense he took Wenger with him. Deprived of income from European competition, Marseille had to start selling their best players in mid-season. At the end of the season, although they still managed to finish second, their sentence was relegation. Meanwhile, even as he reached the Champions League semi-final, that season Wenger ran out of steam in the league and Monaco could finish no higher than ninth place.

'It's difficult to say it's the fault of this or that,' says Ettori. 'We just didn't play that well.' The oddity is that Wenger was in demand. That season the FFF asked him to replace Gérard Houllier as national coach. 'But the national team is six or eight games a year,' says Biancheri. 'For Arsène that's not enough. He likes to come in to work every day.' He refused. (The man who accepted, Aimé Jacquet, went on to win the World Cup in France in 1998.) And then he was offered a job he really did covet.

If circumstances had in the end hindered him from winning as many trophies as his first season promised, Wenger had at least offered Monaco loyalty and stability. Under Tapie's presidency there were eight changes of coach at Marseille in Wenger's seven years at Monaco. One of the changes, briefly, brought in Franz Beckenbauer, fresh from winning the World Cup in Italy in 1990. He stayed for three months. Later, in the summer of 1994, Beckenbauer would contact Wenger in his capacity as president of Bayern Munich, and offer him the job of coach. This was the Kaiser, leader of the team Wenger had seen, among many other occasions, beat Leeds in Paris nearly 20 years earlier, the *libero* on whom he had tried to model himself at the modest level of the French third division. Wenger, with his fluent German and his long fascination with German football, was naturally tempted.

He went to see President Campora to ask to be released from his contract. 'For six years the two of them were like this,' says Biancheri, locking his fingers together. But the relationship had fallen victim to the seven-year itch. Campora may have conveniently forgotten that Monaco attempted to prise Wenger free from his contract with Nancy. Now Wenger wanted to break his contract with Monaco. 'The president said, "No, you're not leaving,"' recalls Jean Petit. 'The president didn't want him to succeed elsewhere.' As at Nancy, Wenger was obliged to cool his heels and stay.

With tidy symmetry, Wenger began his eighth season with Monaco by losing Klinsmann to Tottenham, the club that Hoddle left to inaugurate the Wenger revolution. Klinsmann had been a signing of fitful value. 'He liked it here, but he never really adapted to Monaco,' says Biancheri. His finest hour was a game against Auxerre, coached by Wenger's fellow Alsatian Guy Roux. Auxerre had won the earlier league meeting 4-1 at home. Klinsmann was 'massacred by the stopper', says Biancheri. Wenger complained about the referee, who had sanctioned what he thought were two offside goals. 'When you let four in,' retorted

Roux, 'you keep your gob shut.' In the return at the Stade Louis II, Monaco won 4-0. Klinsmann scored all of them.

For two months of the new season, the team played poorly. Eventually, on consecutive Saturdays, Monaco lost at home in the derby with Nice, then away to Le Havre. Wenger was fired. There was sorrow even at the highest echelons of Monegasque society. 'The princes liked him a great deal,' says Biancheri. 'I think they were disappointed when he left.'

Among the players there was sadness, tempered by the knowledge that these things happen. 'There was a hole when Arsène left Monaco,' says Scifo. 'He was the one who built up the club. He was valued by everyone. But when you stay that long at a club, it's difficult to always stay at the top.'

Only Campora had no regrets, at least at the time. It was the president's decision alone. 'He couldn't consult me,' says Biancheri. 'I was too close to Arsène. But I'm certain of one thing. If you said to President Campora that he could have Arsène Wenger back, I tell you now he'd go looking for him in London in his private plane.'

In the end Wenger's time at Monaco promised more than it delivered, though that was not entirely the coach's fault. In the prevailing circumstances, he had achieved as much as he could. A few months after losing a European Cup semi-final to the best team on the continent, his brutal expulsion was a result less of his failure as a coach than of his hankering for the grander challenge that Bayern would have offered. Campora didn't mind parting with his coach after all, but he preferred to do it on his own terms. According to Daniel Sanchez, one of Wenger's closest friends, he did the honourable thing in staying. 'He could have gone to Bayern but he preferred to stay at Monaco because he thought that he hadn't finished what he had to do there and he could go further. So he was loyal to Monaco and stayed. And then Monaco sacked him. That scarred him.'

After seven years in the wealthiest sanctum in Europe, Wenger was cast into a footballing Siberia.

ÉMIGRÉ

'My life in Japan was so fresh that I can hardly sum up what it meant to me, but every day was totally different from anything I'd ever experienced. Before leaving France, I thought of Japan as a robotised, sad sort of country with no particular attraction. That was mostly due to the European media, which depicts the Japanese as having no life outside of work. I thought they were unhappy people. In fact, it was like going to watch a bad film and then starting to find some good things, and ending up by discovering something wonderful. In the end, my image of Japan was completely reversed. Perhaps I went over the top, but everything seemed good to me. I'd never thought it could be so good. I have a great love for Japan. It has beautiful things that we have lost in Europe, beautiful things that make life good. These are values that we all can use, such as respect for others and for the group, politeness, the ability to be enthusiastic about what you do, the determination to do your best, and respect for the freedom of others in society. The biggest happiness for me was to discover these values in Japan. It felt in some ways as if Japan was my ancestral home. The values I believe in are still being valued in Japan.'

Arsène Wenger

After Monaco, Arsène Wenger turned his face to the east. Trading one royal playground for another, his first stop, in October 1994, was Abu Dhabi in the United Arab Emirates. A series of seminars had long been arranged as part of a push by FIFA to raise standards in coaching around the world. Thanks to his dismissal, Wenger was suddenly available to take part, and he was attached to the seminar held by the Asian confederation. Part of his task was to present a technical report on the recent World Cup in the United States. FIFA had attempted to conquer the continent by allowing America to host the tournament, but football's real newfoundland was Asia. Wenger's audience consisted of coaches from the Middle East, Singapore, Malaysia, Korea, China and Japan.

In the stand at a match the day before the presentation he met an English football journalist called Jeremy Walker, who was based in Hong Kong and editor of the inaugural Asian Football Confederation magazine. That night they went out to dinner. Later, when he arrived in London, Wenger made a point of not forming personal relationships with journalists from English newspapers, nor even distinguishing between them, but he had a couple of questions he wanted to ask Walker. When a few years later Walker attended a press conference at London Colney, correspondents from the national newspapers were astonished to hear Wenger address Walker by any name at all, let alone his first name.

Wenger had been sacked only weeks before, but at dinner in Abu Dhabi he was jovial, relaxed, outgoing, possibly even slightly drunk as he hymned the praises of French wine, especially Chablis. 'It was as if you'd known him for years,' says Walker. 'There was a table near us with two English couples. Arsène said, "Are they from England?" I said, "I think they are from Scarborough." He said, "Do you know them?" I said, "No I'm just guessing." He leaned over and said, "Excuse me, are you from Scarborough?" "No, we're from Hull."' The abstemious Wenger seems to have had a glass or two.

He plied Walker with questions about Japan, and specifically about someone called Stuart Baxter, an Englishman who was coaching Hiroshima Sanfrecce, a team owned by Mazda. There was a reason for this. While in UAE, Wenger was approached by another car manufacturer to come and work in Japan, and he was mulling it over.

'I remember saying that one great reason to go was because the Japanese girls were so beautiful,' says Walker. 'His ears pricked up and he seemed very interested, but in a joking way. Every time I saw him after that, Japanese girls was always his first subject. "Yes, Jeremy, you are right."'

The next day, perhaps nursing a mild hangover, Wenger spoke for an hour in English on the trends in international football he'd observed from USA '94. The tournament was won by Brazil for the first time in 24 years, but in a much less flamboyant style than that displayed by their predecessors, the great team of 1970. His main topic was the demise of the playmaker, the *generalissimo* who dictates the pace and direction of play. Changes in the rules to protect attackers from aggressive defending, and the outlawing of the back pass to the goalkeeper, had opened up play and placed a greater emphasis on speed, power and fitness.

Long before this idea became commonplace, Wenger aired the notion that the team had outstripped the individual. In his estimation the typical new midfielder was a utilitarian link-man who funnelled, tidied and generally minded the shop from in front of the defence and almost never scored. The Platinis and the Hoddles had had their day. Symbolically, USA '94 was the tournament from which the greatest number 10 of the age, Diego Maradona, was sent home for failing a drugs test. The epitome of the thoroughly modern midfielder was the Brazilian captain, Dunga. When Brazil won the World Cup again in 2002, Wenger went out and bought Dunga's successor, Gilberto Silva.

In the autumn of 1994, Dunga and Wenger were simultaneously heading where there was the greatest hankering for the good news of the beautiful game. With South Korea, Japan harboured ambitions to host the 2002 World Cup, and in order to bid were required to set up a professional league. The J-League was born in 1993 with initially ten, then 12 clubs in the top division, all of them company teams which, to give them a chance of currying genuine local support, dropped their commercial appellation and took the name of the city they played in. In Abu Dhabi, Wenger was contacted by Nagoya Grampus Eight, a club owned by Toyota and accustomed to bumping along the bottom of Japanese football since long before the formation of the J-League. They had made a huge initial splash, especially in England, by signing Gary Lineker from Tottenham. When Wenger visited Nagoya's Mizuho Stadium in mid-November for the last game of the season, against Sanfrecce Hiroshima, he was just in time to witness, alongside 21,500 others, Lineker's final, rather forlorn outing as a professional footballer. He was substituted just after half-time.

For a coach who had just taken a team to the semi-final of the Champions League, who had just that summer been offered a coaching job by Bayern Munich, Japan was a left turn into the outback. For players it was a different matter. The cash-rich J League was a gravy train for brontosaurian icons of the world game. Zico, the Brazilian star of three World Cups, had already retired and briefly become his country's inaugural sports minister before he was lured by a move to Kashima in 1991. Lineker followed in 1993, and Salvatore Schillaci, the pop-eyed Sicilian who was his successor as top scorer in a World Cup, arrived a year later. After his brief moment in the sun in Italia '90, Schillaci failed at Juventus and his career went into free fall. Japan was where players like him were starting to fetch up.

But it wasn't where coaches like Wenger went. At 45, he was still young, and yet he voluntarily put himself out to grass in this footballing old people's home. No wonder he had his doubts. He turned over the offer in conversation with old friends. 'He said he thought it was too far from Europe,' recalls Max Hild. Richard Conte, his neighbour and friend from Cannes, says. 'He asked me one day, "Do you think going to Nagoya is the best way to get offers from Bayern, Real, or Barcelona?"'

In the end, Wenger was either very very broad-minded, or too disappointed to care. The truth is that it was a bit of both. For Wenger, going to Japan was rather like joining the Foreign Legion: it was where he could go to forget. He would also be handsomely remunerated in the process. After Monaco, there was an entire litany of tribulations to get over – the brib-ing of three of his own players, the final-year slump in the Championnat, the refusal of his president to let him talk to Bayern, the abrupt termination of his con-tract. 'He went to turn a page,' says Conte.

And yet when he arrived at Nagoya for the first training session in late January 1995 (four days after the Kobe earthquake), there was a reminder of all he had left behind. Dragan Stojkovic was one of several stars flogged off in a clear-out sale after Olympique Marseille were relegated to the second division as punishment for *l'affaire VA-OM*. He was the newly installed star of the Grampus team. Just to compound the sense that Wenger would be working with the enemy, in Stojkovic he inherited the kind of dinosaur he had just declared extinct in his lecture.

After a chronic knee injury that limited his appear-ances in French football, Stojkovic was looking for a well paid deceleration far away from the conflict in his native Yugoslavia. But like most of the imports, he was finding the low standard of play difficult to adapt to. The sight of a slightly long-in-the-tooth European or Brazilian bawling out his Japanese colleagues was common in those early years of the J-League. The problem for Lineker was that his team-mates were simply not good enough to set up the scoring opportunities on which he thrived. Over two years, hugely interrupted by a toe injury, he scored just four league goals which were calculated by one humorist to have cost the club roughly £1 million each.

Stojkovic was not as repressed as Lineker. He rapidly acquired a reputation for having the worst temper in the J-League. In seven years with Grampus he was sent off 13 times. Even Patrick Vieira at Arsenal would never match that. In his first year – pre-Wenger – Stojkovic may also have had reservations about his coach. Gordon Milne was employed on the recommendation of Lineker, who had once been managed by him at Leicester City. He was a flop. Stojkovic appeared not to be trying too hard, most likely because it wasn't going to make much difference.

The footballing year was divided into two stages, one in the spring, the other in the autumn, each named after a different sponsor. In the Suntory series in the spring of 1994 Grampus were eighth out of 12, then slumped to 12th out of 12 in the autumn Nicos Series. The only thing that prevented relegation was the absence, in those days, of a second division.

The directors of Grampus consulted Stojkovic before appointing Wenger. 'I told them that if there was a one per cent chance of getting him to come,' he says, 'they should do everything in their power to make it happen. They asked me why I thought that way. I told them not to ask me anything, but just to bring him and they'd see for themselves. And it turned out I was right.'

As with Monaco, Wenger wasn't his new employer's first choice. Gus Hiddink, a Dutchman who had won the European Cup with PSV Eindhoven, was approached first, but he preferred to take on the Dutch national team. (He ended up coaching South Korea to the semi-final of the 2002 World Cup.) After visiting Nagoya in November, Wenger signed a two-year contract with Grampus worth 75 million yen a year. Before he returned to Japan, his first task was to improve the squad. Traditionally in Japan it was the club who made decisions in the transfer market. It was rare for foreign coaches to be given free rein to sign who they wanted. It was a mark of the trust Toyota placed in Wenger that they limited their involvement to saying that, like everyone else, they wanted a Brazilian. Wenger duly flew to Brazil with Grampus staff to hunt for one, and demonstrated his remarkable eye for pedigree. They looked at various recommended players, but Wenger didn't like any of them. Back at his hotel, he watched a video of another player who had been dangled in front of him. He didn't go for him either but there was a defender on the video he did like. Portuguese being one of the few western European languages he didn't speak, he couldn't understand the commentary, so he went down to reception to ask the name. It was Carlos Alexandre Torres, who happened to be the son of Carlos Alberto, the captain of the 1970 Brazil team.

He also signed the club captain of Cannes, midfielder Franck Durix. Even closer to home, from St Etienne he bought Gérald Passi, an ex-international striker who had scored the winner for Monaco in the Coupe de France final against Marseille in 1991. But his most significant recruit was not a player. It is always said that Wenger spent his time in Japan like a hermit. He was separated from friends, segregated by the language barrier, and away from his new partner, Annie Brosterhous, a statuesque Wagnerian blonde who had played basketball for France in the Olympics. She had a child of her own and could only visit during the school holidays. In fact he didn't travel quite alone. He took along with him an old friend.

In the early 1980s Boro Primorac was playing in central defence for Nice, but also joined Wenger, Conte and Jean-Marc Guillou for two-a-side kickabouts on the beach. Their friendship became public news in 1993 after the Tapie bribery scandal blew up. Primorac was the coach of Valenciennes when three of the club's players were found to have taken money from a Marseille player to throw a league game. Wenger, who had silently suffered an identical fate, had every reason to empathise. It emerged that after the match Primorac had also been approached by Tapie – he had even been to his offices – but after the match in question. 'The first person Primorac opened up to about it was Arsène,' says Jean Petit. It was Wenger who advised him to inform the authorities. Primorac thus became a witness for the prosecution in the trial of Tapie, who denied everything and produced an alibi suggesting that he wasn't in his own office on the day Primorac claimed to have visited him. The two details that convinced the judge that Primorac was telling the truth was his ability to describe the view from Tapie's window, and the fact that he'd noticed Tapie's secretary had very large feet.

It was a potentially suicidal move by Primorac to go public. If his testimony had not been believed and Tapie not convicted, he would never have worked in French football again. The reality is that he never has, but that's because Wenger took him to Japan.

'Boro was in a catastrophic situation,' says Jean-Marc Guillou. 'Arsène said to himself, "I'll take him with me because he has suffered an injustice. I've suffered from one too, but I have the chance to make sure that the injustice doesn't affect us too strongly." Without realising it, Bernard Tapie did Boro a good turn, because he's never regretted following Arsène.'

The season started terribly. Grampus lost eight of their first 10 games. Wenger had never had a losing run like it since Nancy spent two seasons in the relegation zone. Wenger appeared to be another dud European import, like Milne. 'I remember him saying he thought he'd be the first coach in the world to be sacked straight after being sacked from his last job,' says Philippe Troussier, his old friend from the FFF coaching camp at Vichy. Part of the problem was the cumulative effect of defeat. The players didn't know how to win, and Wenger realised that not all his usual tricks were going to work in this foreign culture. For a start, he couldn't get the squad to eat any more healthily, as he later would at Arsenal: they already had an unfatty diet of fish, vegetables and plain rice. He could make them train harder, but Japanese players were so industrious that it was virtually impossible to get them fitter and stronger. Sometimes in training he had to confiscate the balls to stop them over-doing it.

'When he arrived in Nagoya,' recalls Stojkovic, 'we lost seven matches in a row. If Arsène was worried, he didn't show it. Even when he loses, he knows how to hide it.' After the eighth defeat, in which Grampus shipped four goals against Kashima Antlers, he eventually resorted to a last-ditch staple of his at Nancy and Monaco, the exasperated explosion of rage. After the game he shouted at them: 'What are you afraid of? Can you call yourselves professionals playing like this?'

It was an education they needed. There were two things that Stojkovic deplored about playing for Grampus. One was the muddy state of the pitch in the spring rainy season, to which he once drew attention by juggling the ball up the length of the field just because it was easier than dribbling. The other thing was the Japanese indifference to defeat. Where Stojkovic would greet each defeat with sleeplessness and anger, he couldn't help noticing that for all their application in training his team-mates weren't quite so put out when they returned to the dressing-room after another hiding. Via his own interpreter he ranted at the players that winning mattered, that they were not just salary-men in shorts. By the time Wenger arrived, it had started to seep in.

They were miserable about losing, but not as miserable as their coach. When in mid-May a six-week break in the J-League season scheduled for international matches came along, Wenger wasted no time in dragging the team to France. They spent ten days in a training camp at Versailles where he worked on their confidence, encouraging them in concepts alien to the Japanese work ethic such as individualism, risk-taking, tactical adaptability. He taught them that it was no good looking across to the touchline for inspiration when the nature of the game required them to use their initiative, make their own decisions, trust their instincts. Often in the middle of a training game he'd catch them turning to him for guidance, and he'd yell at them, 'Decide for yourself!'

The one thing Wenger wouldn't do to staunch the flow of defeats was tamper with his footballing beliefs. He had always placed his faith in attack and he wasn't about to change. He told the players to keep the ball going forward, and never to pass backwards if at all possible. 'What was very impressive is that we always did the same things with him,' says Stojkovic. 'He never changed his tactics – he had trust in his methods.'

After returning from France, it began to work. Grampus played with aggression, with confidence. They stopped conceding late goals and started to win, and by the end of the Suntory series, they had won 15 and lost 11 and finished fourth. The Nicos series went even better. They won 17, lost nine, and finished second. It was by far the best return Toyota had ever had on their investment in football. By this time, according to Michael Plastow of *World Soccer*, 'They were playing the strongest football that really we'd seen from any Japanese side.'

It was an extraordinary transformation, but the best was yet to come. In the Emperor's Cup, the knockout competition contested after the end of the league season, Grampus were simply unstoppable. On the way they came up against Kashima Antlers, one of the strongest teams in Japan who had inflicted the 4-0 defeat that prompted Wenger to impugn the professionalism of his players. They reversed the four-goal deficit and won 5-1. The final was on New Year's Day 1996 in the Tokyo National Stadium in front of 47,000 spectators. Grampus beat Sanfrecce Hiroshima 3-0.

If Wenger had a reviving effect on Nagoya Grampus Eight, the benefits were mutual. Four years after the seminar in Abu Dhabi, he was at another conference in Paris. It was 1998, and the global footballing community had convened for another World Cup. By now Wenger was at Arsenal, and had just won the Double in his first full season. The conference was two days before the final between France and Brazil in which Wenger would have the satisfaction of seeing Emmanuel Petit, whom as a teenager at Monaco he had nurtured through the death of his brother and then taken to Arsenal, score France's third goal. As the footballing world planned its eastward expansion four years hence, Wenger got up and spoke about how his time in Japan had given back to him his enthusiasm for the game. Jeremy Walker was there.

'He was very down when he left France. The bribery with Tapie and Marseille had really got to him.

He said that from the point where they won the league in '88 it was almost impossible for them to win the league because of what was going on. To go to Japan where the game was still very new and to be treated with respect and have the players who couldn't train enough – they listened and learned quickly – he said his time in Japan gave him back his love for the game.'

There was also something about Japanese culture which agreed with him. Brought up in the Alsatian ethos of workaholism, he came across a comparable mentality in his new squad.

'They were incredible workers,' says Jean Petit, Wenger's assistant coach at Monaco, who visited him in Nagoya. 'If he asked them to get there at nine, they were there at eight. If he told them to run up a mountain, they'd climb it. In France, they'd say, "Why climb the mountain?"'

Wenger wrote two books with the publishing arm of NHK, the national broadcaster. The first came out a year after his move to Arsenal, and concentrated on his experiences in Japan. It was called *Shosha No Esprit*, or *The Spirit of the Winner*. In it he explained how social isolation in Japan had forced him back on his own reserves. He couldn't just pick up the phone to natter to a friend, or slip out for a meal or a movie. 'It made him reflect much more, and made him think about football all the time,' says Plastow, who after 23 years in Japan is as steeped in its culture as any Western journalist. 'He totally concentrated on football. He seems to be describing it as a period of self-discovery.' 'Those two years in Japan were for Arsène a chance to take stock,' says Troussier, 'to set himself back on track and recharge his batteries.'

Japan also appealed to the pedagogue in him. He explained how in France and England a manager only ever meets the players on the training ground, whereas in Japan, out of an eagerness to learn, they sought out his company to talk about football at every opportunity. 'The whole Japanese approach is one of studying football,' says Plastow. 'You get a lot of tactical and strategic diagrams. Wenger was perfectly happy to sit down and talk about technicalities.'

He was even approachable to the press. If Wenger went to Japan both to teach and to learn, it was also a form of vacation from the intensity of European football. It was possible for journalists to saunter over to the dug-out before kick-off to discuss team selection with the coach.

Japan accorded with his sense of social propriety. Wenger had always veered towards formality, and refrained from overt emotional expression, and here in Japan he found an entire race of people who, unlike the French, behaved in exactly the same way.

'He is willing to show goodwill to everyone who shows goodwill to him,' says Plastow, 'and in a very polite society like Japan's where the first assumption is that everybody is showing goodwill to everybody else, and everybody is motivated by the job in hand, it's very attractive to someone like that. There have been foreign managers who've come over and tried to tell the Japanese very directly how to do everything and they don't succeed at all. Wenger is a man who's happy to work in a system and the system in Japan is such that provided you do work within it you are allowed to do anything you like. It sounds contradictory but it's true.'

One of the things he got away with was making his own decisions about signing players without interference from the boardroom. But the main thing he got away with was extracting himself, without animosity on either side, from his two-year contract.

The second season began with another trophy, the Super Cup, in which Grampus beat J-League champions Yokohama Marinos 2-0. Wenger said that while his challenge in the first season was to reinforce the concentration of a team used to losing, in the second season it was to do the same with a team used to winning. It worked. They carried on where they left off. But something nagged at the coach. For all his success, there was a lurking sense that, in the end, the J-League was not the real thing. He started to pine for Europe, for a higher level of competition, for football with deeper roots.

'He missed the established nature of the passion,' says Plastow. 'It was just after the J-League had begun and the Japanese crowds were fantastic but they didn't really know quite what they were doing. It was more like Disneyland than Highbury.'

This mattered less in the first season. Wenger had had several approaches from European clubs, reassuring him that he had not been forgotten. Almost as soon as he arrived in Nagoya, he heard from Werder Bremen. There was a symmetry to this. When Wenger was refused permission to go to Bayern Munich the previous summer, the Bavarian club went to Bremen instead and hired their coach, Otto Rehhägel, who had won promotion and two Bundesliga titles and beaten Wenger's Monaco side in the Cup Winners' Cup final in 1992. Although Bremen's president and general manager flew to Nagoya for talks with Wenger, he couldn't possibly wriggle out of a contract on which the ink had scarcely dried.

There were other offers in 1995, but in the second season they petered out. In *Shosha No Esprit* he explained how he was torn. The choice was to sign an extension to his two-year contract that would send out a message to European clubs that he had no immediate interest in returning, or to leave. With his larger ambitions not yet fulfilled, the idea of losing touch with Europe gnawed away at him. So he stopped his Japanese lessons and started to listen to offers.

In the summer there was an approach from the FA in England. The country was enduring an emotional June hosting the European Championships, at the end of which the national side lost its coach Terry Venables, who resigned after the semi-final defeat against Germany to deal with an impending court case. His successor was Glenn Hoddle, one of whose first moves was to recommend the man who had revived his career, and given him his only championship medal, for the post of FA technical director. But Wenger was not remotely interested in withdrawing from daily contact with a squad of players. There was also an approach from Racing Club de Strasbourg. Gilbert Gress, who was coach when Wenger joined the Racing staff in their championship-winning season in 1978, had just left after his second, much less

successful period in charge. Wenger was tempted by
the prospect of a prodigal son's return to Alsace, to
the club closest to his heart, and serious negotiations
ensued. But he already had a spoken agreement with
another club.

Wenger first met David Dein, the vice-chairman of
Arsenal, in the late 1980s when he attended a game as
Dein's guest at Highbury. They also met in the south
of France, where Dein had property. According to a
rival Premiership owner, thre was one thing above all
that caught Dein's eye. 'It was the name,' he says. 'He
just loved the name.' Tickled pink by the idea that
someone called Arsène might come to Arsenal, Dein
tracked his progress and, by the time he was eventually approached by the club, Wenger was able to refer
to Dein as 'an old friend'.

That first approach happened a whole year before
Wenger actually agreed to join Arsenal. After nine
years they had just sacked their manager George
Graham for financial irregularities. Dein proposed
Wenger to the Arsenal board, but could not persuade
them to go out on a limb. Bruce Rioch was lured from
Bolton Wanderers as, it turned out, a stop gap. A year
later, even before Rioch was actually sacked, Dein
went back to the board and this time was much more
forceful. By now, Chelsea had promoted their senior
foreign player, the dreadlocked Ruud Gullit, to take
over from Hoddle as Chelsea manager, so Dein's colleagues were persuaded that Arsenal would not be
taking too reckless a step.

Wenger nonetheless recognised it as a huge leap of
faith for Arsenal. He was acutely aware that only one

foreign manager had ever been brought in to manage an English club, and that wasn't a success. Dr Josef Venglos (who subsequently turned up in Japan) lasted just one season at Aston Villa. Wenger was immensely flattered. Among the people he called for advice was his mentor Max Hild.

'He phoned me to tell me that he'd had contact with Arsenal. I said, "Don't hesitate, it's the most respectable club in England. And it's a club that's very well known in France because it always came to play in tournaments in Paris." *Les Cannoniers*, we call them in France.'

Wenger was still pondering his next move when word slipped out in the European press. He thus found himself in the awkward position of being asked to break a contract with six months still to run in a country where contracts are generally respected. Grampus offered to raise his salary to 100 million yen, but if money wasn't the reason for coming, it wouldn't be the reason for staying either. Wenger had been here before. In his previous two jobs, he asked to be released from his contract. Both Nancy and Monaco said no. In each case the mooted job was with a bigger club, and Wenger's employers refused to be intimidated. In Plastow's opinion, this situation was slightly different.

'Wenger had turned the team around in a remarkably short time and was assuredly regarded as the most successful foreign manager in Japan to date (and probably still is). There was tremendous respect for him and his judgement, and also the hope against hope that he might come back one day. At the very least, the club would have wanted to retain the good relationship for use in the future. In addition, Wenger had always behaved honorably and built up a fine personal relationship with the players, officials and staff. Everybody liked him, so there wasn't the will to stand in his way when the move was so obviously a good one for him. Perhaps there was also an inferiority complex: how could a club like Grampus pretend to compare with Arsenal? The offer was simply too good for Wenger to resist, and everyone here agreed with that. Wenger had earned the right through his comportment to be treated with the same consideration as a Japanese. There is no higher praise.'

Jeremy Walker caught wind of the rumour concerning Arsenal early. He met several British journalists in July, on a pre-season tour of the Far East by Kevin Keegan's Newcastle United, who had just signed Alan Shearer. The third and final match was in Osaka, and Wenger was in the executive suite next to the media box where Walker watched the game with ten or so English football reporters. 'I said to them, "I'll introduce you to the next Arsenal manager." They said, "Who's that then?" "Arsène Wenger." "They'll never fire Rioch." I said, "Let's just wait and see."'

Wenger's first exposure to the British press was a positive one. He confided to them that he had been approached by the FA, but that he'd turned the job down in order to stay in club football. He seems to have charmed the journalists rotten. 'They all thought he was completely different,' says Walker. 'When you've had managers being rude to you for years and years and talking to you like you just don't deserve to be in the same room, to have someone like him so educated and so well mannered, they thought, "Wow, I hope he is Arsenal manager."' The next encounter wouldn't be quite so enjoyable.

A month or so later Wenger had used all his diplomatic skills to extricate himself from his contract, not in time for the new English season but long before the end of the Japanese one. Walker called him at his home in Nagoya. 'I thought then he'd had a few. He came across as very upbeat and very funny. He'd just got it sorted out. He seemed very relieved it was all over. He'd managed to come out of it looking really good.'

At his final game Wenger thanked the fans in such Japanese as he had managed to learn before he gave up his lessons. Little did they know that he had tried to get Stojkovic, the club's best player, to come to London with him, but the Yugoslav refused. (He also offered Stuart Baxter a job as his assistant, but according to Walker, Baxter said that 'he didn't think that Arsène's assistant would do much more than collect the balls in the string bags'.) For all the fans' reciprocal gratitude, Wenger left behind him a mixed legacy. Grampus finished the season second when it was felt that, under Wenger, they would have won the title. Just as before his arrival the club had never had a sniff of success, so after his departure more or less the same squad of players reverted to type, even when Wenger recommended his close friend Daniel Sanchez as coach a couple of years later. Another recommendation had more impact. When in 1998 the Japanese FA were looking for a coach to guide them to the

World Cup four years hence, Wenger suggested Philippe Troussier. Troussier stayed for four tempestuous years, at the end of which he unexpectedly led his team into the second round. As a pundit, Wenger was welcomed back by a commercial Japanese station to commentate on Troussier's progress. He sat in a studio offering cursory comments through an interpreter while either side of him hyperventilating presenters and guests clowned about. Sheer excitability was a side of the Japanese personality he couldn't ape.

RÉGIME

'The Arsenal offer came through an old friend. England was the birthplace of football. There was only one previous example of offering such a job to a person like me, who had never played in England, a country with over a century of football history. That's only natural. With a history like that, it was almost unthinkable to turn to an outsider for help. It was like Japan turning to France for a sumo manager. I'd be only the second manager from outside going to an English club team. That was a big attraction and challenge. This offer really appealed to me.'

Arsène Wenger

In August 1996, the name Arsène Wenger meant absolutely nothing in north London. 'Arsène Who?' ran the *Evening Standard* headline that greeted his appointment. It was the story of his life, from the moment he took charge of his own team at Nancy, 12 years earlier. In every new job, he didn't just have to prove himself; he had to introduce himself. 'I remember when Rioch was sacked one of the papers had three or four names,' says Nick Hornby. 'It was Venables, Cruyff and then at the end Arsène Wenger. I remember thinking as a fan, I bet it's fucking Arsène Wenger, because I haven't heard of him and I've heard of the other two. Trust Arsenal to appoint the boring one that you haven't heard of.'

Nick Hornby is sitting in San Daniele, a trattoria in Highbury, up the hill and round the corner from the famous old ground. The walls of the restaurant are adorned with the black and white regalia of Udinese, a small-town club from north-eastern Italy. This is the dining-room of the Arsenal establishment. After mid-week home fixtures an entire aristocracy of Arsenal fans convene here to chew over the game and generous bowls of pasta. Hornby sits at one table with his crowd, Melvyn Bragg with his at another. They are all tucking in by the time David Dein arrives with Arsène Wenger, and possibly Patrick Vieira, plus wives, girl-friends, an assortment of agents, directors and sundry others from the footballing shadows, to take their seats on the other side of the room. When Wenger enters they stand up and give him a ten-second ova-tion. If Arsenal have won, that is. But then if they haven't, he doesn't come, not even when they baked him a cake for his 53rd birthday. Arsenal had just lost at home to Auxerre. Wenger was so distraught at the defeat he locked himself in his office and, despite Dein's entreaties, wouldn't come out.

Hornby's bestselling book *Fever Pitch*, about the psychopathology of the football fan, and the Arsenal fan in particular, was published at the height of the George Graham era. The book saw in two league championships, and a lot of grinding football

characterised by hair-trigger offside traps and domi-
neering one-nil wins. It turned Hornby into, by some
distance, the best known Arsenal fan and the most
widely read football author in Britain. When they
met, Wenger had actually heard of both writer and
book, published in French as *Carton Jaune* (or
Yellow Card).

'He said, "Ah! You wrote *Carton Jaune*. Why no
other book?" I said, "I have written some other books
since." "And it's OK? You can live from writing?" I
said, "No no, things are going fine." It was beyond his
conception that you would want to write anything
other than a football book.'

Arsenal went for a man with no other life outside
football. Wenger was a hermit whose altar, once he'd
settled into his new detached home in Totteridge, was
a large flat-screen television on which he'd watch a
never-ending flow of matches deep into the night. But
because his personality presented such a blank canvas,
there were those, usually thought to be Tottenham
fans scared out of their wits, who decided they could
paint on it what they wanted.

No sooner had Wenger set foot in England than a
grotesque rumour swiftly mushroomed on the inter-
net that the new saviour of Islington had a highly
deviant sex life involving not only women, not even
just men, but also children. Without repeating the
content of the rumour itself, newspapers passed on
the fact that a rumour of a plainly damaging nature
was in circulation.

According to one eye witness, Wenger was 'incan-
descent with a white hot rage' when he heard about it.

But at least in France one of these rumours was in fact old hat. 'During the seven years we were here we were always together, except at night, and people thought we were homosexuals!' says Jean Petit, his assistant coach at Monaco, and one of his closest friends. Wenger immediately called Petit in France.

'When the tabloids were behaving as if he was a paedophile, he said, "Listen, go to Roquebrune," where Annie, his wife, lived. Annie had a child from her first marriage. He said to me, "I think they are in front of the house. If they're there, if they see Annie, they are going to think..." So I went. There were loads of people there. I said to Annie, "Don't go out."'

There was a home game for the reserve team that day. Fans were gathering outside the stadium, and they congregated around a group of press, some football writers, other news reporters, and a television news team, who were waiting outside the stadium for an official comment from within the club. Meanwhile, inside, it was made clear to a distraught Wenger that in England he could not simply sue the newspapers for libel unless they specifically published the charge made against him. He did, however, rapidly take on board, when it was explained to him, that he could sue for slander if any of the reporters outside could be persuaded to put a name to the rumour in front of witnesses. Against the advice of Dein, and to the alarm of the press officer Clare Tomlinson, whose own first day in the job this was, he went outside onto the steps of Highbury's famous old marble hall and confronted them.

This was an act of considerable bravery. According to Tony Adams, Wenger 'hates confrontation', and here was a confrontation before he had taken charge of a single game. For all the press knew, he was about to resign. Instead, he asked them why they were there. When someone referred to unspecified rumours, Wenger said, 'What rumours?' No one spoke. The journalists, feeling hampered by the presence of the fans, asked if they could come inside the stadium and have a private press conference. Tomlinson refused. Facing the realisation that they had nothing to go on, the press slunk away. Wenger had killed the story stone dead, although one Sunday newspaper did phone him to advise that they would be publishing a series of highly compromising photos the following weekend. With estimable sangfroid, Wenger urged them to get the evidence out earlier in order not to be scooped, and put the phone down. After his pleasant encounter with the football writers in Osaka, it was the worst possible introduction to the English press on their own patch. A few weeks later, it emerged that his partner Annie was expecting his first child. A girl, Léa, was born in the summer of 1997. (In May 2004, after 38 unbeaten games, she paraded on the Highbury pitch with her father.)

On the football pitch, it was easier to get the measure of Wenger, even before he'd actually arrived. As at Monaco, his first signings turned up ahead of him. They were both French, which was a giveaway for anyone like Hornby still hoping the new man would be Cruyff. One of them was Rémi Garde, from Racing Club de Strasbourg. He spilled the beans when he told the press that he was looking forward to working with Wenger, even though Wenger was at this point still officially the coach of a club on the other side of the world.

'It was peculiar because he was in Japan,' says Hornby. 'I couldn't understand what a top-notch manager was doing there. It seemed very odd. It seemed like he'd already failed in European football and had been farmed out. Winning the French league with a team that had money didn't seem to be a startling achievement. The thing that changed it for a lot of fans was Vieira.'

A bit like a prophet, Patrick Vieira announced Wenger's coming when he emerged as a substitute against Sheffield Wednesday. He had been kicking his heels in the Milan reserve team, and Arsenal were the beneficiaries of his long-stifled desire simply to play meaningful football. 'It was just apparent immediately that this 18-year-old was something extraordinary,' says Hornby (who exaggerates the player's precocity: Vieira was in fact 20). 'He completely changed the game and dominated it the moment he came on. I think that really excited people's interest in the manager, that he'd done something very smart very quickly.'

Did they but know it, the influence of Wenger had been felt a whole year earlier. According to Laurence Marks, the comedy writer who was working on a book about Arsenal in Wenger's first season and is also a close friend of Dein, the vice-chairman took advice from the man he had wanted to bring to the club in 1995. Although he has always been seen as

Rioch's signing, it was Wenger who urged Dein to make a move for Dennis Bergkamp, who at Internazionale had failed to get used to a weekly diet of negative tactics and claustrophic attention from man-to-man markers. No one, as Wenger had proved with Hoddle and Hateley, was better at spotting the players on the international market who'd leap at the chance to get away from clubs where they were stagnating.

'I believe, through talking to David Dein,' says Marks, 'that it was Arsène Wenger who advised David Dein to get Bergkamp to Highbury. That purchase was not made by Rioch.'

Because they didn't know who he was, one Saturday two weeks before his arrival Wenger appeared by live satellite link on the video screens at Highbury. They should have played it in the dressing-room too. It was one thing for the club's most famous fan not to have heard of Wenger, quite another for the club captain. Like Hornby, Adams didn't know the new man from Adam.

'There was a feeling of who the fuck is he and what is he going to do? What is he?' says Adams, who first heard tell of Wenger when he got a call from the club chairman, Peter Hill-Wood, ringing from New York. Rioch had been sacked, caretaker manager Stewart Houston had left for QPR and Adams and Rice were 'kind of just getting on with it', recalls the captain. 'I got a call from the chairman along the lines of, "I hear the shit's hit the fan back there. Er, don't worry, rally the troops. Good man on his way. Be patient." It was quite hilarious.' (It's a toss-up which is dodgier: Adams's Etonian accent or his Alsatian one.)

Did he know anything about Wenger? 'No.' Literally the name meant nothing? 'No. Nothing at all. He wasn't an English top-of-the-tree coach with proven experience. He wasn't an Alex Ferguson. He wasn't a renowned manager of that time. A George Graham.'

Wenger's appointment was announced on 20 August, he met the press on the 22 September and took official charge on 30 September, a Monday morning. 'He arrived unnoticed at the training ground,' Lee Dixon recalls. 'A meeting was called, the players filed in and in front of us stood this tall, slightly built man who gave no impression whatsoever of being a football manager.'

Dixon had been absent injured when Wenger briefly met the team the week before. In one of those quirks of fate that football likes to throw up, Arsenal were halfway through a two-legged UEFA Cup tie with Borussia Mönchengladbach, the team Alphonse Wenger took his young son to see. Thus Wenger met the team for the first time in Germany, at a ground he'd known for more than 30 years. Pat Rice, the assistant coach, was in charge of the game. At half-time the aggregate score was 4-3 to Borussia when Wenger walked into an Arsenal dressing-room for the first time. He switched the defence from a back three to his preferred option, a back four, and Arsenal promptly lost the tie. After the match Adams vented his spleen at Rice. 'I was absolutely livid,' he says. 'David Dein wheeled him in to the dressing-room, where he was supposed to have had no involvement, took over at half time, changed the team and consequently got us knocked out. I was just about to rip the guy's head off. I turned round to Pat Rice and said a few Fs and thought, how dare he? It was my first experience. Obviously when he became the manager we had a talk. Sunny day at London Colney, sitting on a bench, and we spoke at length.'

Adams says that Wenger wasn't a George Graham. That was precisely why the club hired him. Graham's crowning achievement was to win a championship in 1989, famously in the dying seconds of the season, with a side impressively crammed with graduates from the youth team. Success went to the head of some of the young champions, notably Paul Merson and Adams, who by the time Wenger arrived were both recovering alcoholics. The pair of them had started to mend themselves, and it was Wenger's job to mend the club, to wean it off the amateurish notion that you could drink copiously (and eat randomly) and still be a professional footballer.

Even though he was even more teetotal than Wenger, Adams made fun of his new boss's puritanism. He recalls a typical exchange.

'I'd say things to him like, "Arsène? Take the boys away?" And he'd say, "Yes, we go to training camp?" I said, "No, we used to go away to Marbella and get drunk for five days." "No! We go away, we go to training if you want." "No, no you've missed the point. We go away, we play golf, we get drunk, we fall over, we have fights." "Oh that is incredible. You used to do that?" "Yes, we used to go out drinking straight after the game and get home Monday, come into work drunk." "No I don't believe that. You played at 70 per cent of your capacity! It is ridiculous that you are still playing."'

If a culture of gambling and drinking had attached itself to the club, there was worse: Graham was sacked, and banned from managing for a year, after he was found to have taken money from an agent in the signing of players. It wasn't even as if the players were any good. In his final seasons, the football was horse-tranquillisingly dull, epitomised by the negative capabilities of Danish midfielder John Jensen, whose winning goal in the European Championship in 1992 had fooled everyone into believing he was the embodiment of verve and adventure. He wasn't, and nor were Arsenal. In four years he scored for Arsenal just the once.

'With George everything was predicated on winning,' says Hornby. 'If they weren't winning anything, there was absolutely nothing to watch. It was so dismal watching that team 20 times a season. They were awful.'

'George had a fantastic group of youngsters that he controlled and we achieved great things,' says Adams. 'That squad broke up in '92, '93, and we didn't have the second wave. With a very very average squad we won the European Cup Winners' Cup with a fantastic attitude, work-rate and fantastic defending. It was an enormous effort. That team was ready to bust. I personally was not able to kick another ball. I was at my lowest point. The club was pretty much going nowhere. We were all ready to jump ship.'

It was an extremely precarious moment in Arsenal's history. With Manchester United now dominant, Arsenal had become entirely dependent on an impregnable defence and the goals of Ian Wright to keep them in contention. 'There was no reason why we couldn't have turned into Spurs after Rioch,' says Hornby. 'People seem to think it's part of the natural order of things that Arsenal and Man U are one and two in the Premiership more or less every year now. It's not in the natural order things. It's entirely because of Wenger.'

Arsenal was the job Wenger had been waiting for all his footballing life. It was a culmination of everything, a validation of the choice he had made all those years ago to amass an encyclopaedic knowledge of every conceivable aspect of the game. He felt he had come to the home of football, where the connection between the fans and the team trounced anything he had thus far experienced. In Monaco there were no supporters to speak of anyway, and in Japan fanaticism was only skin-deep. His first games at Highbury, with the small see-through dug-out so close to the fans, assaulted his senses, and those of all the French players he brought in.

If Wenger had waited for this job, he had also prepared for it. Many of the changes he effected at Arsenal were previously road-tested not only at Monaco but also at Nancy. This being an old club, however, with entrenched traditions, he understood that he couldn't change everything at once. When he arrived, Wenger chose to drive the club forward with a mixed economy of revolution and evolution. He reassured players that some things were going to stay the same, even as others changed out of all recognition. The first decision he took was to persevere with most of the existing squad, and specifically the existing defence. The famous back five of Seaman, Dixon, Adams, Bould and Winterburn had already clocked up hundreds of hours together, and racked up countless clean sheets, but they were nearly all the far side of 30. Despite the fact that at Monaco he had signed the 32-year-old Patrick Battiston, Wenger believed that that was precisely the age a footballer could no longer hack it at the top.

Adams, who was pushing 30, recalls that 'he would say things like, "Physically a professional footballer is finished when they are over 30. It is not possible to play at that age." He believed that players over 30 were dead. Steve Bould, Lee Dixon and Nigel Winterburn proved him wrong. They proved that with desire, commitment, and by looking after themselves, they could play well into their 30s at the top level. He acknowledged that and let them do it instead of getting rid of them. If you are in a beautiful house you don't go moving to a terrace. That's what he realised.'

There were casualties, though. John Hartson, the kind of rugged forward Wenger would happily have inflicted on French defences, was sold to West Ham. He was unsuited to the kind of football Wenger was interested in deploying to slice through Premiership defences: Hartson could do power, but he couldn't do pace. Merson, kept out by Bergkamp, eventually departed for Middlesbrough.

Later, another fading Arsenal icon, Ian Wright, was successfully manoeuvred out. By the end of the season a second French teenager had arrived from Paris Saint Germain, this one a coltish 17-year-old called Nicolas Anelka, and at the start of the next, there were two more of his compatriots, whisked away from Wenger's former employers at Monaco: Gilles Grimandi was one, a sturdy utility player; the other was Emmanuel Petit. He also dipped his toe back in the West African market. Declining to spend a fortune to bring his old discovery George Weah from Milan, he thought he'd have a stab at moulding his cousin Christopher Wreh instead.

Thus within a year of Wenger's arrival, French had become the second language of the dressing-room, much as English was at Monaco with Hoddle and Hateley. By the end of Wenger's first full season, the Arsenal team was a pantomime horse. The back five was entirely old and English. The front six was mostly young and French and, with the arrival of Marc Overmars to play alongside Bergkamp, Dutch. The Francophone influence deepened over the years with the purchase of Thierry Henry from Juventus and, after the French victory in the European Championships in 2000, Robert Pires from Marseille and Sylvain Wiltord from Bordeaux. Around this time, Wenger also started to indulge his taste for the more efficient Brazilian players in Silvinho, Edu and Gilberto Silva.

Wenger encouraged all his foreign players to learn English, the language in which he gave team talks. But the training ground was further gallicised by the hiring of Boro Primorac and a coterie of drop-in French health and fitness gurus – Yann Rougier, a specialist in dietary supplements, his assistant Hervé Castel, and osteopath Philippe Boixel.

They were a colourful bunch. One of Dr Rougier's other business ventures was the marketing of a herbal remedy to enhance sexual performance. Boixel specialised in a very French and not always scientific brand of lateral-thinking cures when faced with a complex injury problem. In an effort to cure troublesome Achilles tendon injuries, players might have the alignment of their wisdom teeth checked by x-ray or tomatoes removed from their diets. When Garde went to him with a problem with his groin, Boixel noticed an imbalance in his sight that was causing him to run incorrectly. He prescribed contact lenses. Adams's problems with his right side were ascribed to a car crash in 1990 when he dislocated his toe. When his form was affected by a problematic ankle halfway through Wenger's first full season in charge, it was too serious for Boixel to sort out. Wenger flew him down to the Côte d'Azur for a week to work with a fitness specialist called Tiburce Darrou. After his knee injury, Pires went there too.

Meanwhile, Wenger's friends and former colleagues dropped in from France: Jean Petit, Jean-Luc Arribart, Claude Puel, Henri Biancheri, Daniel Sanchez, above all Jean-Marc Guillou, with whose club KSK Beveren Wenger arranged a deal to send young players out to train. Puel, who subsequently won the Championnat as Monaco coach, reports that 'since his time at Monaco Arsène has progressed a lot in the level of his training. He has even more variety and even more structure than in his time at Monaco.'

It wasn't that French was suddenly the *lingua franca* of the training ground. But the thinking was in French. Wenger more or less overlooked Arsenal's existing medical staff (although both were working with the England national squad at the time), one of whom was a dermatologist, the other was old enough to retire, and neither of whom had any qualification in sports science. Most of the Arsenal old guard never learnt the surnames of the newcomers. One of them thinks that Boixel's surname is Boxal. After seven years of working with him, Adams refers to Primorac as 'Boro Piveral, or whatever his name is, the coach or whatever he is.'

Mystery shrouded Primorac even within the club. Wenger's closest ally was a silent type who did not fraternise with the players much off the training pitch. 'He is a hard man,' says an insider. 'He is a very funny guy at times. There are people who say, "What does he do?" He watches every tape ten times over. He watches football morning, noon and night. He is Arsène's eyes on the world game. He is an encyclopaedic reference to almost any player in the world.'

Some of the players may have assumed that the innovations were all Wenger's doing. In fact they were common practices on the other side of the English Channel, and even in other power-oriented sports in Britain, such as athletics and rugby. Wenger inherited two players who had captained England. One was Adams. The other, David Platt, had spent four seasons in Italy and seen it all before. 'There were one or two players that were frightened,' says Platt. 'They'd heard of training three times a day, and strict diets. The likes of Patrick Vieira and myself knew that wasn't the case. These were continental ideas, not Arsène Wenger's. I'd been used to four years of good advanced work. So I was looking forward to Arsenal going continental.'

Opinions vary within the squad at that time as to how firmly the changes were imposed. In his book *Safe Hands*, David Seaman recalls, 'He told us, "This is how I run training and this is how I expect you to eat and look after yourselves."'

Platt says it was subtler than that. 'He changed nothing immediately. That's where he was clever. Slowly but surely he implemented his methods. I think Arsène would have preferred not to have given a day off during in the week. If you're playing on a Saturday you have Sunday off but then you're in Monday to Friday. But he didn't do that. He was very very clever. He'd get the youngsters in but older players he'd give a day off in the week. He sold that as "The younger players can train; the older players need the day off." Load of crap, to be honest with you. He'd have preferred to have them in Monday to Friday.'

The first specific change was on the morning of his first game in charge, away to Blackburn. The squad trooped into a ballroom in their hotel and, for half an hour, stretched. Wenger introduced protracted warm-downs after training and matches. 'We would stretch after every training session,' says Platt. 'We'd go back into a room at the training ground and stretch for 30 minutes. I hadn't seen that in England. The morning of a game we'd get up and instead of going for a walk we'd stretch.'

Adams was already a devout stretcher, but it was a novelty to some of the other players. In came a masseur (amazingly, an English one) to adminster balm to aching muscles. Wenger took the holistic approach. The whole player needed to be prepared for games. Everything contributed, from specific attention to specific muscles, through the more general application of sensible diet, to vaguer environmental improvements. Wenger was dismayed, for instance, by the low-rent premises of the training facilities outside St Albans which the club shared with University College Hospital.

'I remember being introduced to him on the first morning he came to our grounds at London Colney,' says one coach. 'There was no office for the manager. He was shocked that a club of Arsenal's status was renting it and had done for however many years.' Wenger immediately withdrew the squad to Sopwell House, a swanky hotel five minutes away by coach. It was here that they changed, showered and, most importantly, ate for the next two years.

Nutrition was another area where change was necessary. Wenger arrived from Japan, where he'd spotted that there was almost no obesity. The staple diet of boiled vegetables, fish and rice was perfect for a footballer. In an ideal world the entire squad would have turned Japanese on the spot. But he understood the maxim about taking horses to water. 'He didn't come in and say, "Eat this,"' says Adams. 'At no one stage has he ever done that with anything. He just laid it in front of us.' This is not entirely true. When the script-writer Maurice Gran was returning on the same plane as the team from a game in Athens, 'We all had to eat same appalling food,' he recalls. 'Boiled chicken with no flavour whatsoever and boiled broccoli with less flavour than the chicken. This was the famous Wenger diet.'

The central tenet of Wenger's nutritional philosophy was pretty simple: if you eat a sticky toffee pudding, you'll play like one. He talked to the players about slow sugars and sweet sugars. But sugar was not the only blacklisted foodstuff. He also frowned on red meat, eggs, chips, baked beans – a caricature of the English footballer's staple fuel. His dietician came in and explained the benefits of pasta, boiled chicken, steamed fish, raw vegetables and water. He even tinkered with the order in which players actually consumed their food.

'For years Loughborough has been telling me to put carbohydrates in first,' says Adams. 'The doctor would say, "Try putting protein in before the carbohydrates."' Wenger also practised what he preached: apart from the odd pudding, he kept to a low-fat diet.

Pasta, which boosted energy levels, was the pre-match dish Wenger preferred the players to eat. But again, he stopped short of insisting. 'He was open enough for you to go to him and say, "I don't want to do that,"' says Platt. 'Nigel Winterburn wasn't used to having that kind of pre-match meal and Nigel went back to poached eggs on toast. Arsène was fine with that. He wasn't dictatorial in any way. It was suggested.' Once more, none of this was entirely new to all the Arsenal players. Adams had been introduced to a book by Robert Haas called *Eat to Win* as far back as 1987. 'We were always concerned about our diet,' he says. 'It just so happened that I would be going out on a Saturday night and putting 30 pints of lager down my neck over the weekend.'

There was also a choice when it came to taking vitamin injections and dietary supplements, specifically creatine, a naturally occurring protein which, if taken during heavy training, can boost energy and reduce fatigue. Again the choice was take it or leave it. Adams, who had owned up to his alcoholism only a week before Wenger's arrival, was not inclined to put anything foreign into his body.

'I would never take the creatine. I didn't take vitamins or B12. He tries to say, "I want you to be the best athlete you can possibly be to play for this club. These are the pills if you want to take them. This is the regime that I want you to eat. Don't eat chocolate. Get to bed early." He'll lay it in front of you but he won't tell you.' Others did take the creatine, and found that they could maintain a level of performance deeper into a 90-minute game than previously. Those who joined the England squad gossiped about the changes, to the consternation of Wenger, who sought to maximise any advantage he could gain over the opposition.

On the training pitch he was equally secretive about his methods. Wenger believed that he was bringing something new to English football, but naturally he wanted there to be only one beneficiary.

Players subsequently writing autobiographies kept details to a minimum. Wenger's interest in the science of training had been born 25 years earlier in Strasbourg when he had debriefed his professional friends about sessions at the Racing training ground. By the time he got to Arsenal, his ideas were fully formed.

As usual, Wenger was the first to arrive and the last to leave, even though as an English-style manager rather than a French-style coach he was now able to delegate more. Pre-season fitness training was overseen by fitness coach Tony Colbert, warm-ups by Rice and Primorac. The training sessions themselves found Wenger at his most dictatorial. This was one area where he was able to make the horses drink. Like an athletics coach, he ran things by the stopwatch. He reduced the number of distance runs, and replaced them with intense timed runs and bleep tests. 'There was specific running, sprint work,' says Platt. '30 seconds on, 30 seconds off. It was just very very organised and very detailed.'

To the annoyance of the players, games were timed to the second – no more than ten minutes each way – and if they ended in a draw there was no golden goal, but penalties. All ball work, with players in a circle passing and moving, was also timed to the second. The same went for sprint work. When the goalkeeping coach Bob Wilson prepared Seaman and the reserve keepers, he would know his time was up when Wenger called over and said, 'Bob, you've got two minutes.' Which meant 120 seconds. According to Martin Keown, 'We don't overtrain by a minute. It's all timed scientifically.' A typical session would last no more than 45 minutes. It would finish with a run around the pitch.

One area where timing was applied even more strenuously was in a form of muscle-strengthening exercises known as plyometrics. Wenger first came across isometrics when playing for Mulhouse in his mid-20s under Paul Frantz. Isometric exercises, mostly used in the first stages of rehab, are a form of muscle-strengthening exercises that don't put any strain on the joints. Plyometrics involve much more strain but produce vastly more dramatic results. Long used by sprinters, hurdlers and jumpers to build up power levels, the exercises were new enough to English football that Wenger had to demonstrate them himself. They involved sudden ballistic movements in the form of bounding exercises – hopping, skipping and jumping. Wenger used them to top up the conditioning of super-fit players in the midst of an endless blur of matches. As they required a protracted recovery period, he could use them only if there was no midweek game. Typically he'd do this in internationals week. Before he arrived, those not selected to play for their country would get three or four days off.

'Arsène wouldn't do that,' says Platt. 'He'd give you a couple of days off, but he'd also give you two or three days which was almost like a mini-pre-season.' Platt explains the science of plyometrics in layman's terms. 'The contraction of the muscle gives the energy. When your muscle contracts, it's like a coiled spring: you've got more energy going up it, rather than when it's at full extension. If you stand up and you jump, you won't jump as high as if you jump up and down a couple of times very very slightly and really go for it. You wouldn't be knackered from it. It is very heavy work on your muscles and yet you don't really feel the work.'

It didn't take long for Arsenal's players to become the fittest and leanest in the Premiership. More specifically, Wenger's training produced players who were able to peak at the appropriate moments in the season – what sports scientists call periodising. The famous run-in in the spring of 1998 was a triumph of periodisation. Arsenal were literally stronger at the death.

This was the truly revolutionary part of Wenger's regime. The odd thing is that the revolution was bloodless. 'I've never seen a player lose it with Arsène,' says an insider, 'where I've seen players lose it with every other manager I've ever seen.' There are two reasons for that, one of them obvious: results. These scientific preparations translated, less than two years after his arrival, into the Premiership and FA Cup double. The second reason was Wenger's reward for the first. University College Hospital were going to have to find new tenants. Arsenal were moving to a new training ground.

The new palace was built at a cost of £12 million, paid for out of the protracted sale of Anelka to Real Madrid in August 1999 for almost twice that sum. It was the kind of facility Wenger had originally tried to secure for his players at Monaco, but which failed to materialise in seven years. Now at London Colney, backed by a board that was prepared to believe in him, he started all over again. The building was designed more or less to his specifications, and inhabited according to his rules. These largely revolved around hygiene. When people enter the main ground floor they are required to take off their shoes and put on flip-flops provided. At the other end of the building there is a separate exit and entrance to the pitches beyond. When players come in, they remove muddy boots and kit and put on white towelling dressing-gowns and flip-flops. No mud is allowed through the 'dirty room' and into the building.

It's consistent with Wenger's obsession with secrecy that the training ground at London Colney is impregnable – a bit like the back four which Wenger inherited when he arrived at Arsenal. There is no way through to the inner sanctum for anyone who has not been given security clearance. But this is what it looks like. The building is shaped rather like a boat, and is on two floors. The feel of the place is futuristic, like something by Norman Foster. There is glass and natural wood everywhere, plus the inevitable framed photographs of great Gunners moments, all of them in the Wenger era. The ground floor is divided into two sides. One of them is entirely given over to the Academy, with school rooms, a computer area, and extra changing rooms for visiting teams and referees. The other side has the senior administrative area, including Wenger's office and the coaches' changing room. Further down is a huge and impressive American-style locker room for the first team, which has capacity for up to 30 players. The lockers are generous in size. Beyond that is an anteroom where they put on their boots before going out to train. On their way back in, when they emerge from the 'dirty room', there is a big shower room with meaty shower heads, as well as a steam room.

There is an extension where the visiting nutritionist Yann Rougier has his office, next to the physios' area. There is a large gym. The middle of the building contains the medical area, the beds, the Jacuzzi and a swimming pool with the moveable floor. The depth can be adjusted from six inches to five foot five, giving an injured player scope to run in shallow water or, if he mustn't load an injured foot, knee or ankle, there is the option of strapping a float to his back and running without touching the bottom. The float can be finely set if the player needs to bear at least some load. All along one side of the pool is a window. According to Wenger, leg injuries can be better observed and diagnosed when a player is walking through water. The pool has floor-to-ceiling windows looking out on to pitches.

The pitches themselves seem to go on forever. They are all in pristine condition, like golf greens, meticulously flat and, in the case of two of them, undersoil-heated. Such was Wenger's attention to detail that he instructed the club groundsman to prepare pitches of exactly the same dimensions and texture as the playing surface at Highbury.

After training the players repair upstairs, which is one vast room containing a restaurant, and sofas for catatonic slumping. The first team eat at one end, the Academy members at the other. Wenger personally selected soothing pastel shades, rather than the fierce club colour of red, for the walls. There is one other room upstairs. It is a makeshift press room for those days, usually Fridays, when Wenger talks to journalists before the weekend game. But it is also where tapes are screened. They are prepared by Prozone, who will supply video illustrations of the tactics of opposing teams. Prozone also film Arsenal, and two days after every game there will be tapes on the desks of Wenger, Rice and Primorac containing a complete breakdown of every short run, long run, header, shot and pass of every single player.

Only the carpark is potholed. Knowing Wenger's determination to leave no base uncovered, perhaps they are in precisely the same size and configuration as some potholes outside Highbury.

It is the personal fiefdom of one man, a testament to the faith that the board of the directors have in Wenger and the magic he can conjure every time 11 men run onto a football pitch with the image of a cannon on their shirt. No one in the history of English football has ever done more, by way of preparation, to ensure that his team are not firing blanks.

And when the players go home, Wenger remains. He stays till past six every night, which is not late for a banker but is for someone who watches more football at home and then works all weekend. He finds the time to tend to his own fitness. When he first arrived at Arsenal he would walk, but in the summer of 1999 he had an operation on his knee and later he got back into jogging and swimming. On the morning of a game he swims at the team hotel. He never, under any circumstances, joins the players, either in a round of golf, which he doesn't play, or in the practice games. But every so often, he likes to kick a ball. Sometimes he will wander over to where the goalkeepers are coaching and decide to join in. He pings shots into the corner, bending, driving, lifting the ball beyond the reach of his keepers. 'Technically he may not be the world's greatest player,' says one of his coaches, 'but his knowledge of what part of the body to control the ball, how to play the ball, how to run with it – you would have thought he was Johann Cruyff.'

GUNNER

'Arsenal has been in existence for 130 years. The Englishman supports his club in every sense of the word. Loyalty is the key word in English football. The public never whistles at or attacks their players. A club is for life, and it's a daily topic of conversation. When my team loses, I can't help thinking about the unhappiness that we are creating in so many families. Even at birth you can surround your baby with items in the image of your favourite club. There are even huge mail order catalogues.'

Arsène Wenger

'You would be amazed by how little the man does. But that's his strength.' Tony Adams proposes meeting in the kind of watering-hole he now favours: Starbucks in South Molton Street, slap in the middle of Mayfair. When he removes his huge tweed coat you fully expect him to be wearing... but no, for some reason, underneath it he's not wearing a red shirt with white sleeves.

In the first year of their separation, Adams's adjustment to life without Arsenal had fewer hitches than Arsenal's adjustment to a life without Adams. At first they seemed to be getting along fine without him. In the autumn of 2002, Arsenal produced Harlem Globetrotter football: they made the opposition look like dupes; they played for fun, and Thierry Henry was the best striker in the world. The team had voyaged to a higher plane where there was no real need to think about the mundanity of prevention, the yeomanry of defence. They were far too busy describing complicated geometrical shapes in and around the opposition penalty area. They played football that, by general consensus, had never been seen in England before. Mainly because it wasn't English. It was football from Venus, the game played with a terrible, irresistible, logical beauty.

But that was the autumn. In September someone asked Wenger if the team could go the whole season without losing. Wenger thought it was something to aim for. By Easter, the time of the year when obduracy and resolve and nerves of reinforced steel are called for, they were misquoting that line back at him. The defence that Adams had marshalled for 15 years started to ship unnecessary goals – a free header for Giggs at Highbury, an own goal at Villa Park, a late pair at the Reebok, the three to Leeds that conceded the championship to Manchester United. As Arsenal haemorrhaged points, and lost irreplaceable players to injury and suspension, both men must have been thinking the same thing: if only the captain's legs could have withstood just one more year.

Adams is tall, rangy, charming and, unexpectedly, rather handsome under his shaggy tinted hair. There is an undeniable aura about him, undermined only slightly when he pokes a big finger into his empty mug, scrapes the cappuccino froth off and licks it clean. 'I'd give my kids a slap if they did that.' He grins boyishly. He'd do no such thing.

It was largely a coincidence that Adams announced his alcoholism to the press at London Colney just days before the arrival of Arsène Wenger. But the two events seemed to lock arms, and alchemise someone seen as uncultured as both a player and a man. Off the pitch, the alcohol-free Adams embarked on a long and as yet unfinished journey towards self-reinvention. He started going to the opera, and using the word 'spiritual' a lot. He went back to school and at the same time lectured football squads all over the country on the perils of addiction. On the pitch, Wenger freed him from the yoke that George Graham had placed on his shoulders as a teenager, gave him permission to express himself too, to come out and play. Wenger had the same liberating effect on Lee Dixon and Nigel Winterburn. He told the back four that they had been stifled, and that they must now be themselves. He gave them an Indian summer.

And yet, in spite of the amount that he and others owe to Wenger, Adams is clearly resistant to the idea of overpraising the Wenger era, because it subtracts value from the achievements that went before. Adams won two championships under Wenger, but he and the rest of the back four also won two championships under Graham, and he is proud of them. They all are. 'Arsène still considers that George Graham suppressed the '91 team,' he says. 'That's between him and George. I think the '91 team is as talented as any squad that Arsène Wenger ever had and should have done the Double that year.'

In a way, Graham won half of another championship in 1998 and a third of one in 2002, because half the team that won the Double in 1998 had been drilled and drilled into the most efficient defensive unit that English football has ever seen, and they were mostly still there four years later. On the other hand, that defence was part of a team that had done nothing in the league for the four years before Wenger's arrival. The two managers had very different footballing creeds. Graham was not unlike a totalitarian centralist who pared the liberties of his players down to the bone. Wenger was a sort of free-market liberal who left everything up to individual choice. The difference was there in how many instructions they gave to the players. Graham's teams went onto the pitch like squaddies rucksacked with too much information. Wenger's teams have always travelled light. And none lighter than Arsenal.

According to Adams, a manager can do only so much anyway. He cites an American study of coaches and champions conducted over 20 years. 'Champions,' he says, 'have got to have 100 things, and ten of them are to do with the coach. So Arsène has to do 10 per cent for me to be a champion.' Whether you accept the arbitrariness of that fraction or not, the fundamental point is that a coach has to accept the limitations of his role. Once the players take to the pitch, a thin white line painted on the grass separates the manager from further usefulness. He has handed the reins over, and surrendered himself to the rule of an array of variables over which he has no control: these include luck, fate, the referee, the rub of the green, the mood of his French centre forward, of his Dutch play-maker, of the opposition as a unit and as 11 individuals. A manager's job is to reduce the influence of the variables. It's part of his ten per cent, and no one works harder at the ten per cent than Wenger.

Some of that ten per cent was achieved by the imposition of training routines and dietary rules in the mood-enhancing environment of swanky new premises, designed to maximise the potential of each player in the squad. No one's players were as physically and mentally prepared as Wenger's.

But then there was the moment they actually ran onto the pitch. The best way of reducing the variables, clearly, is acquiring players superior to anyone they are likely to encounter in the opposing team. In football this has always been expensive, and around the time Wenger arrived in Britain it was becoming exponentially more so. In two ways Wenger was lucky. He was lucky to inherit the most durable defence in the history of English football. He didn't have to buy another defender for a couple of years. And he was lucky, as well as skilful, in the transfer market. He was offered the job at a specific moment in the history of world football when an entire generation of meticulously nurtured French players were about to mature into World Cup winners. Some of them had even been nurtured by Wenger at Monaco. This generation wanted to pursue their ambitions with clubs bigger than any in the French league, to be paid higher salaries and play in front of larger crowds, and the thought of working with a Frenchman was attractive. Back then there was no Gérard Houllier, no Jean Tigana to lure their compatriots to Liverpool or Fulham. So although he could never have afforded Zidane, the best of them all, as the most high-profile French coach working outside France Wenger was well placed to pick off all the (relatively) cheap ones. And by the time he came to sell those who wanted to leave, he had made them into much better players, and he brought the club huge profits – most spectacularly via Anelka, bought for £500,000, sold two years later for £23 million.

Jean-Marc Guillou talks about Wenger's nose. 'It's being able to have a sense for these things. There are coaches who judge potential better than others. And just as there's the knowledge of the player, there is also the knowledge of his situation. He saw that Vieira and Henry left France too young. Going to Italy is not easy. They get there at 20 in a club full of stars. It's difficult to break through. But on the other hand they make progress because they are watching great players. It was a great coup getting players who weren't too expensive. He liked Pires for a while before he bought him. He got him at the right moment. He got him when he was lowest.'

Patrick Vieira set the template for almost all Wenger's most successful signings over the years, and even the unsuccessful ones. He was young, French, gifted, and unhappy – in Vieira's case at Milan. Petit was ready to move on from Monaco. Henry was unhappy at Juventus. Pires was unhappy at Olympique Marseille. Anelka was unhappy at Paris Saint Germain (*plus ça change*...) Wenger kept an eye on the transfer market, and pounced. He used a similar tactic to lure Nwankwo Kanu, out of action at Internazionale after heart trouble, and Davor Suker, out of favour at Real Madrid.

At the same time he was always sifting. He took a punt on any number of players he thought he might be able to mould into something. There is a long list of faces which turned out not to fit. Christopher Wreh was an experiment that largely failed, though he did score a small but vital number of goals in the Double-winning season in the spring of 1998. Luis Boa Morte, it emerged, was better suited to lower altitudes. And then there was the Latvian, Igor Stepanovs – proof, according to one wag, 'that Wenger is human'. Stepanovs, signed after Wenger flew to Riga in a private jet to watch him play, was in the front line when Wenger suffered his worst result yet at Arsenal: 6-1 away to Manchester United in March 2001. He even took a punt on Junichi Inamoto, the first Japanese player to be signed by a Premiership club, though he scarcely ever played him, and got rid of him soon after he had starred in Philippe Troussier's 2002 World Cup team. Other players, mainly French or French-speaking, drifted through. At any one time there were always several of them on trial at London Colney. 'He gets a lot of people over to find the gold,' says Adams.

Wenger first started moving players out of position at Nancy. He had learnt to trust his instincts. As far as he was concerned, positioning was negotiable, and he saw things in players that they had not previously been encouraged to see in themselves.

At the end of the season in which he took over, Arsenal missed out on second place, and a Champions League qualification, on goal difference. He responded by signing Marc Overmars from Ajax and Petit. Petit had started out under Wenger at Monaco as a left back. Like a knight on a chessboard, he now moved across and forward into central midfield. Overmars was also converted from a winger into a left-sided midfielder. When Henry arrived, he too thought of himself, somewhat glumly, as a winger. But Wenger needed a pacy replacement for Anelka. He shifted Henry into the middle and patiently waited for him to locate the barn door. Usually it took several months for the players to believe in themselves the way Wenger appeared to.

Later still, Wenger started converting a series of utility midfielders into standby full backs: Lauren, van Bronkhorst, Touré. (He was less interested in spending money on defence.) The most extraordinary transformation was wrought in Ray Parlour, an old-school Romford boozer with no pace or left foot. The new diet turbo-charged him, and Wenger moved him from the middle out onto the right flank, where his one-footedness would be less out of place. He even worked out that Parlour's control of the ball was accelerated if it arrived at a certain angle. He told the other players to make sure they delivered it into accurately into his stride.

Whoever the personnel, wherever they played, Wenger had to fold them into a system. 'He likes 4-4-2,' says Adams. 'He thinks that works. He likes splitting lines. That's about it.' In his introductory press conference Wenger said as much. He said he liked speed backed up by technique, and getting the ball forward early. But he was reluctant to be too dogmatic. He had videos of Arsenal's Premiership matches couriered out to Nagoya while he waited to take over. The team he saw on tape played with Rioch's preferred system, a three-man central defence, and for the first season he was persuaded by the players to stick with it. The willingness to be flexible ran parallel with a sense of relief that he was back among battle-hardened pros who didn't need to be held by the hand. He had just spent the best part of two seasons telling Japanese players exactly what to do, and he wasn't about to do the same in England.

'He would have to get much more involved in Japan,' says Adams. '"Tony, I have to teach the boys in Japan. I have to tell them how to kick it to the right. I'm not going to tell Lee Dixon to pass it there. He has the ball, he's an intelligent player, let him go play. What do I tell Tony Adams about defending? What can I tell Thierry Henry about goal-scoring?"'

In *Safe Hands* David Seaman says, 'It was not so much that players were being told to do this and that but more that they were not being told not to do things.'

In fact, this governed Wenger's entire style of leadership, certainly in the area of tactics. Instructions to the team, both on the training pitch and in the dressing-room, were reduced to the barest essentials, partly thanks to the manager's belief in non-intervention, partly due to the fact that half the team didn't speak good English. And then they were reduced even

further by his ability to get his message across economically. 'His instructions are so clear,' says an
Arsenal coach. 'So many managers need 20 minutes
to get their point over. Arsène will do it in ten words.
It's a charisma. Before charisma it's intelligence. The
guy is so succinct and so simple. He will do it visu-
ally. He will put people in the positions.'

It also helped to shave minutes off his addresses to
the team that he was never too bothered by the opposition. A short video was shown to the squad the day
before the game, but attendance was optional. His
inclination was to leave them out of the picture altogether.

'He never talks about the opposition,' says Adams.
'"What has the opposition got to do with it? We play
free, we move the ball." If there's something obvious,
he'll say, "They have a big centre forward who flicks
the ball this way to the right winger who is very
quick." It may be a little reminder. Straightforward,
clear, short, quick, simple instruction.' Adams says
team talks before a game lasted no more than five
minutes and they would contain a maximum of six
points – three defensive, three offensive. He may occasionally refer back to the previous game. In his book,
Footballeur, Pires says the team talk lasts seven minutes. 'Any longer and he reckons it would be counterproductive... He underlines the strong points on
which our defence and attack should lean, what we
should be doing at corners, who should take free kicks
and penalties. It's all very compressed and to the
point. For him, football has to be a game everyone can
understand.'

When he arrived at Arsenal, Wenger was slightly taken aback to discover what he described as a 'party atmosphere' in the dressing-room, with loud music blaring, Parlour cracking jokes, often in an Inspector Clouseau accent at the expense of the new manager, Martin Keown pumping himself up vociferously, and Pat Rice shouting his head off to motivate the players. Wenger had the cultural sensitivity to understand that there was no overpowering need to change any of this. Before a game his own style was to remain almost disturbingly calm. This wasn't the case only in Japan, where journalists could collar him ten minutes before the game for a chat. 'I went to Highbury for the match against PSV and asked to see Arsène,' says Enzo Scifo. 'One hour before the match he came to see me, really at ease and relaxed even though he had a big game.'

Lord Hollick had a similar experience at Tottenham, where he was dining with the Arsenal board of directors before the game. 'Arsène was one of the people around the table. Someone said, "Clive has been very much involved in setting up the Euro campaign." Arsène immediately took an interest in this. We engaged in a very detailed conversation. He had a very impressive grasp of the arguments for and against the Euro, including harmonisation of tax, which he discussed in a confident and relaxed manner. It was rather like a couple of students having a conversation at university. (He is pro-Euro with significant and sensible reservations.) Our discussion went on for quarter of an hour. I looked at my watch and said, "It's 25 minutes to go. I don't want to keep you." He said, "I think they know what to do. There is no need for me to rush down and give them another briefing." I was struck by his charm and intelligence and his grasp of the intricacies of the issue – he's thought about it, that was the impressive thing – but also his relaxed demeanour in front of what was a crucial game. He was totally confident that his team knew what was needed. It was a mark of calm confidence.'

At half-time he will be equally quiescent. He'll check for injuries and after that insist that everyone sit quietly and say nothing for most of the interval. It is Wenger's belief that no one will be in a fit state to listen for at least ten minutes. If Rice is bursting to let off steam about something, Wenger asks him to be quiet. With three minutes to go he will make a few brief points. 'He would draw our attention to details on the pitch,' says Dixon, 'encourage us, talk of patience and passing, and that would be it.'

Wenger doesn't blow his top if he can help it. Opinions of those closest to him vary about whether his rare flashes of anger are strategic or spontaneous. 'Arsène does not shout,' says one witness within London Colney. 'It's not his way because he believes you can only do it four times a season, perhaps five at most. If you are continually screaming at players, they just say, "Here he goes again."' Gilles Grimandi noticed that the Wenger who had coached him at Monaco was not quite the same as the Wenger who had signed him for Arsenal. 'Gilles tells me he was a very different man,' says Adams. 'He was a very angry man and his team talks were very very volatile. He used to shout quite a bit.'

His most famous eruption was during that wipe-out at Old Trafford. Both Dixon and Adams missed it, but then if they hadn't been injured there would probably have been no need to explode. According to Pires, Wenger 'went berserk'. He later told the press that Arsenal had played like a youth team. What he said at half time must have been spontaneous because they were already 5-1 down: no tactical outburst was going to make any difference. The game was over and, although it was only February, so was the championship.

Adams remembers a previous thunderstorm from the first game of the same season, a 1-0 defeat away to Sunderland, in which the referee sent off Vieira for retaliation just before the final whistle, while his opponent Darren Williams had clearly overreacted to provoke just such a miscarriage of justice. 'He came out with, "The referee! That is unacceptable!" That is the level of his anger.' By the following week Wenger had been charged by the FA for 'alleged threatening behaviour and physical intimidation', after the fourth official claimed that he had been manhandled by Wenger in the tunnel. He was threatened with a 12-match ban and a fine of four weeks' wages. The touchline ban was subsequently overturned.

Dixon, likewise, has one collector's-item memory of a half-baked Wenger tantrum. 'My only experience of Arsène's anger was during one half-time. He came into the dressing-room, clutching a paper cup. You could see he was angry. He screwed the paper cup up, and threw it into the bin, but missed. The paper cup fell helplessly on to the floor, and the impact of his message was lost.'

It was Dixon's opinion that Wenger does not go berserk enough. 'There were times when the senior players at the club were privately willing Arsène to have a go at certain players for not pulling their weight, There were times – Tony Adams and I talked about this – when we felt things should have been said after games. But he does not believe in saying things in the heat of the moment. Even on a Monday, after a poor Saturday, when we were waiting for him to say something, nothing would be said. That silence often said more. He left it to you to figure out.'

'He wouldn't bollock you,' says Adams, 'and he wouldn't say you're the best thing since sliced bread. He's not a Kevin Keegan.'

The overall picture, in short, is of someone who has reduced coaching to a form of Japanese minimalism. But he must have been doing something right because the football at Arsenal changed overnight. Nick Hornby remembers the sheer speed. 'They just played three times as fast as I've ever seen an Arsenal team play before. There were three players in that team – Overmars, Vieira and Anelka – who could break from one penalty area to the other in ten seconds. It was just like they'd become turbo-injected. People just loved it straight away. It was like, "Oh I see. Why doesn't everyone do this?"'

The team finished third, but there was little hint after nine months of what was to come. They could have studied the form book and noted that at Nancy, Monaco and Grampus Eight, Wenger always had his best season first. But this was England, and Manchester United had won four out of the five first Premiership titles.

By December of 1997, there was no hint that Arsenal might be on the cusp of breaking the monopoly. Bergkamp had scored a miraculous hat trick against Leicester, but still the team had drawn. When Blackburn out-muscled Arsenal at Highbury the team was booed off the pitch and, after four defeats in six games, Wenger didn't appear to have the answers.

'There were a lot of Wenger doubters that month,' says Hornby. 'I don't think anyone would have given tuppence for their chances of winning the Double. At that stage it was a doubt about the quality of the players that were being brought in. They were a shambles. The defence looked old and exposed. Overmars looked like a busted flush and a one-trick pony. Petit just did these little left-foot dinks towards the forwards.' Worst of all, Adams looked frail and out of touch.

Wenger had a three-hour meeting one afternoon with Adams in which they did nothing but drink cappuccino. It was a rare opportunity for Adams to bend the manager's ear. 'He hates confrontation. He will listen to you when you pin him down. "Actually, Boss, I need to speak to you." "Yes, I will speak to you next Wednesday." "Boss, it's Wednesday." "Can we do it Friday?" You can never fucking pin the guy down. Once you do get him he'll listen.'

The best place to get him is on a plane. Adams remembers one conversation on a flight home from Newcastle. Wenger had panicked in the second half, taking off a midfielder and sending on a defender. Newcastle equalised. 'On the plane coming back I said, "Don't be afraid to not do that. Let us handle five or six people. It doesn't matter how many people are in my zone. I could manage ten." Sometimes he panics. "Sugar! I need to put another defender on." I just said, "Trust in me, trust in the players, we can cope." He always accepts that. I couldn't have had that conversation with George.'

Soon after their three-hour talk, Wenger called a team meeting at Sopwell House. Adams complained that the midfield was giving no protection to the defence. Other players threw in their hap'orth. The air was cleared. A Christmas party swiftly followed at the Café de Paris, where the two halves of the team bonded. Adams went off to Antibes to get his ankle seen to. And Vieira and Petit started playing as a tel-epathic midfield unit. Petit said that they could have played together blindfolded.

And yet the transformation was not instant. While the captain was away Arsenal began their assault on the FA Cup by drawing 0-0 at home to Port Vale in the driving rain.

After that result, it would be impossible to guess that within four months Wenger would have led his team to the Double. Adams returned to the team at the end of January, armed with a specific instruction from Wenger to remind the rest of the team that he was captain. Promptly before his first game back Adams had a go at Bergkamp. 'You've been over here two and a half years,' he said. 'Isn't it about time you won something?' There was no one better at building a player's confidence, and inspiring his loyalty, than Wenger. He told Vieira he was going to be one of the best midfield players in the world at one of the greatest clubs and, though Vieira frequently threatened to leave, he never did. As for dressing players down, it was as if Wenger was using someone else to do his confrontation for him.

Arsenal stuttered towards the FA Cup final via two penalty shoot-outs while devouring Manchester United's vast pre-Christmas lead in the Premiership with a sequence of ten wins, culminating in a 4-0 demolition of Everton. Wenger's praise for his players, at Goodison Park and at Wembley, was as usual temperate. David Platt has no memory of Wenger's reaction to winning the Double.

Adams says he 'spends too much time in his head. I keep on at him. "Come on, boss, show me some emotions." He intellectualises his emotions. Once you do that you try and control them. He's frightened to let go. I think it's intellectual repression.' One of the reasons why he could not give way to unadulterated joy was because he was always thinking ahead to the next campaign. This is the man who once said he'd far rather not have summer holidays.

In his first full season, he had won two cups rather than one, but it is nonetheless remarkable how Wenger's fortunes at Arsenal mirror those of his time at Monaco almost identically. As in France, in England he was at the second best club in the country, and for the next three years his team finished second best, just as Monaco mostly did to Marseille. As at Monaco, he even led Arsenal to a secondary European final and lost. (And their richer rivals Marseille, like Manchester United, won the Champions League.)

A year on from the Double, it was still very close. In the Cup semi-final replay against United, Bergkamp missed an injury-time penalty that would have won the game. Then on the final Saturday of the season Arsenal had to rely on Tottenham, now managed by George Graham, not losing at Old Trafford. Mystifyingly, Graham took off his best player, David Ginola, after four minutes. The summer brought a serious crisis, with Anelka ungratefully jumping ship to join Real Madrid, leaving Wenger to spend the first half of the next season bedding in Henry with which-ever partner was best suited to him. In the winter Arsenal were a distant fourth, but won eight league games in a row to finish second again. In the summer of 2000, while France were winning the European Championships, there were more departures for Spain. Petit and Overmars, who arrived together three sea-sons earlier, left together for Barcelona. The joint sale, for £26 million, confirmed Wenger as a peerless inves-tor, but necessitated another season of transition. This time it was Pires, Wiltord and a young left back called Ashley Cole who needed to be accommodated. Thus in 2001 there was a third consecutive runners-up place, but this time Manchester United won by an emasculating 18 points. That year Wenger led Arsenal to the inaugural FA Cup final at the Millennium Stadium in Cardiff. The other finalists were Liverpool, coached by Gérard Houllier, an old friend and rival who owed his appointment to Wenger's success in England. Arsenal went ahead with a goal from Freddie

Ljungberg, only for Michael Owen to score twice for Liverpool in the last ten minutes. It seemed as if Arsenal were turning into perpetual bridesmaids, just as Monaco were.

For Wenger, there were two differences. There was no corruption in English football, or nothing as organised as what he had experienced in France. Like Olympique Marseille, Manchester United had money on their side, but they used it in the transfer market, rather than covertly in the black market of bought results and thrown games. And there was automatic qualification for the Champions League for the side finishing second in the Premiership. So long as he finished in second place, Wenger now had annual access to the best European competition.

For the club's first two years in the Champions League, the Arsenal board decided to maximise revenue by playing at Wembley. The capacity was almost doubled, so that there were suddenly 70,000 Arsenal fans. And yet it was counterproductive. Rather than cowing the visiting opposition, it inspired them. Arsenal made a habit of drawing games that they should have won. Throw in their dismal record away from what they temporarily called home, and they twice failed to qualify for the second stage of the Champions League. The first year it was the distinctly undaunting trio of Lens, Dynamo Kiev and Panathinaikos who thwarted them; the second it was Fiorentina, Barcelona and AIK Solna.

'Wembley hindered us,' says Adams. 'We felt like we were playing away from home and you've got no advantage. Arsène was a little bit annoyed. The board are very powerful and they'd done it as a money-making enterprise and some would say it worked for them financially but it was detrimental to the team and as soon as that outweighed the financial stuff that the board were getting they agreed to take it back to Arsenal.'

After failing in the Champions League that second year, Arsenal went into the hat for the UEFA Cup and duly progressed to the final. It was an echo of past journeys for Wenger. On the way Arsenal beat Werder Bremen, who had offered him a job while he was in Japan, and who had beaten Monaco in the final of the Cup Winners' Cup in 1992. The final in Copenhagen was against Galatasaray, Monaco's conquerors in his first year in the European Cup. In his only previous European final, the players had not been themselves after learning of the collapse of a temporary stand in Bastia the day before, causing 18 deaths and over 2,000 injuries. This time, his players seemed rattled by the violence that preceded the match, and in the stadium by the uniquely intimidating atmosphere created by the Turkish fans. The match went to a penalty shoot-out, at the Galatasaray end. Arsenal had already gone out of two competitions on shoot-outs that season, and now they lost a third.

In the autumn of 2000 Arsenal went back to Highbury for their Champions League games against Shakhtar Donetsk, Sparta Prague and Lazio. The combination of a weak group, home advantage, and growing European nous got them through to the second group stage for the first time. They lost away to

Spartak Moscow, squandered a 2-0 lead at home to Bayern Munich, a game in which Wenger vented his frustration by falling out with the fourth official (as he allegedly had at Sunderland four months earlier). They finished joint second with Olympique Lyon and scraped through to the quarter final on better head-to-head results in their two games with the French club. They thrillingly beat Valencia, the previous season's beaten finalists, 2-1 at home, but lost 1-0 away and were out for another year.

By the start of the 2001-02 season, Wenger and Arsenal had won nothing for three years. On a positive note, this was the first summer he didn't have to sell any of his prize acquisitions. But one of them, Vieira, whom Wenger had moulded into one of the best players in the Premiership, was getting itchy feet. Real Madrid were mentioned. So were Juventus. So were Manchester United, or at least they were by Alex Ferguson. Wenger offered Vieira an olive branch by making him captain in the absence of the injured Adams, and although he was spotted in Madrid as late as January of the ensuing season, he was eventually persuaded to sign an extension to his contract. Acknowledging the coming break-up of Arsenal's defence (Winterburn and Bould were long gone), he finally spent big money on a defender. For the second time in his career, he signed Tottenham's best player. This time it was Sol Campbell.

The Champions League took the same course as the previous season. Arsenal progressed past Schalke 04, Panathinaikos and Real Mallorca, and the second group produced a splendid 3-1 home win over Juventus, in a group also containing Deportivo La Coruña and eventual finalists Bayer Leverkusen.

By early March 2002, after Bergkamp had scored a miraculous goal of the season against Newcastle, Wenger announced that he thought Arsenal were capable of matching Manchester United's treble of three years earlier. He turned out to be two-thirds right. Pires had played well enough to win him the Footballer of the Year award, but a cruciate ligament injury removed him from the second stage of the Champions League, and Arsenal failed to reach the quarter-final. In Europe, at least, they had gone a step back. But domestically, they were playing the football of Wenger's dreams – fast, intricate, direct and unstoppable. Ljungberg came into the side and con-jured up enough goals to power Arsenal to the cusp of both the Premiership and the FA Cup. One of them was a wonderful curled shot at the final in Cardiff against Chelsea, which they won 2-0.

Arsenal went to Old Trafford for the penultimate game in the Premiership having not lost a single league game away from home and needing only one point to win the title. Wiltord scored the winner, and Wenger rated this second Double as his greatest achievement in England. Manchester United fans cer-tainly thought so. The majority of them stayed after the whistle to applaud the enemy as they lapped the pitch. The trophy was given to the players at Highbury the next week. The squad bowed down in only semi-mock reverence to a plaster-casted Pires. It was Dixon's last game for Arsenal. And although he had yet to make an announcement, it was also Adams's.

A few days later Adams visited Wenger in his office at London Colney. 'I went and saw him and thanked him for the six years I'd worked under him and said, "The greatest gift you've given me is to let me perform my stuff. You showed me great respect." It was quite emotional. He didn't say a lot. He never does. He thanked me for the service I gave him. And we hugged and I walked out the door.' It was the end of one of the greatest odd-couple partnerships.

In the autumn Adams and Wenger met again at a funeral. 'He came up behind me. "Hello? How are you?" I said, "I am unbelievably well. Physically never felt better. Haven't got to abuse my body any more." "Yes? You have lost weight." I said, "I've lost a lot of muscle definition." "Yes, you have lost a lot of muscle definition. How is your weight?" I said, "I am actually the same weight, would you believe, because I've changed my diet." "You are happy because you finished at the top." Off. That was it.'

MANAGER

'Arsène Wenger is somebody I would like to get to know better. People who do know him tell me he is a good man but I don't suppose I'll ever find that out for myself. He seems to pull down the shutters when you meet up with him and he never has a drink with you after the game.'

Alex Ferguson

'I don't know whether he likes me or not. I don't know him well enough and those things don't worry me.'

Arsène Wenger

In 2001, the newly knighted, treble-winning Sir Alex Ferguson announced his impending retirement. 'Alex has done marvellously well,' Arsène Wenger said as Arsenal pursued their second Double under him and Ferguson prepared to leave, 'but his club has such potential they will continue to be tough, no matter who comes in after him. It will not be a relief when he retires. They have the money to buy a good manager, the money to buy good players. It will go on. United have twice our budget, but I don't envy that because I enjoy our rivalry.'

This was typical Wenger. 'Wenger has got this great way of making a gently barbed comment but dressing up as if it's a bouquet of flowers,' says Henry Winter, the football correspondent of the *Daily Telegraph*. In this case, on the surface he pays Ferguson a compliment. But the closer you look you see that he has actually belittled his relevance to United's triumphs while drawing attention to his own lonely poor man's struggle to match them.

There is a short story by W. Somerset Maugham set in a Swiss sanatorium. It tells of a pair of elderly male in-patients who have turned their loathing for each other into a way of life. Their sniping antipathy grows out of the fact that one of them, according to the other, has the superior room. One day, unexpectedly, the room's owner dies, and his enemy contentedly moves in. But something is wrong – not with the room; the room is fine. Something is missing. He is pining for his old foe, the man who, it turns out, has defined his existence, who has given him a reason to live. Without that reason, he also dies.

When Ferguson first announced his retirement in 2002, Wenger would not have been human if he did not start eyeing up the superior room. But it never happened. Ferguson had a change of heart. Perhaps he couldn't bear the thought of Wenger moving into his room. And perhaps Wenger was relieved Ferguson didn't go; perhaps, back then, he would have pined without him.

No one knows the true answer to any of these questions, possibly not even the two men themselves. But theirs has been a compelling and peculiarly complicated relationship from the moment Wenger set foot in England in September 1996. It was not a relationship in any ordinary sense. They scarcely spoke to each other. Wenger, notoriously, did not accept Ferguson's hospitality. The actual physical contact was restricted to shaking hands twice a season, once in Stretford, once in Islington, plus whenever they meet in the Charity Shield (1998, 1999, 2003) or the FA Cup, as they did in 1999 (famous for Giggs's wonder-winner), 2003 (famous for Giggs's baffling miss), 2004, 2005 and 2008. In 2000 there was also one worthless encounter in the Worthington Cup (Arsenal 4 United reserves 0). But it was still a relationship. It's just that it was conducted entirely through an interested third party: the media.

It's easy, therefore, to present their rivalry as a media invention. 'Arsène has no rivalry,' says Tony Adams. 'It's myth, it's media speculation. When Arsène says something he says it honestly. If anyone does, Alex Ferguson uses psychology. He will say things and Arsène will say things. He hates confrontation and he wouldn't go out of his way to manipulate a fight or a psychological battle with Alex Ferguson. He's too busy watching videos; he's too busy working on the team. It's complete crap, it really is. He's not remotely interested. But when he's asked the question, like "Why didn't you have a drink with him after the game?" Arsène will answer honestly. "Well I have to get back on the coach and go home with the boys." Arsène blanks Ferguson. He's not interested. They get on like any other managers. There is respect there and that's it.'

It may be easy, but it's not the whole story. The media has merely been, if you will, the medium. Now that it's all over, it would be possible as part of a media studies degree to write a thesis on the way in which Ferguson and Wenger conducted their long-distance affair, their megaphone marriage. It developed, over the years, into something wonderfully absorbing. Part of what made it absorbing, and enlightening, is the way Wenger has told himself and the rest of us that, at least for him, it was not a personal rivalry at all.

Asked once if Ferguson might actually dislike him, Wenger said, 'It doesn't really take my sleep away.' When Arsenal were presented by fate with the chance to win the Premiership at the home of the holders in 2002, he even claimed that 'winning the title at Old Trafford will have no special significance'.

When Adams says that Wenger 'has to do his ten per cent to make me a champion', that ten per cent involves giving the team the best possible chance of winning: buying players, ensuring they are as fit as possible, encouraging them to play in a certain way. But it is also the job of a manager to communicate with football's outside world, to talk into the microphones and dictaphones fanned out in front of him. This has nothing directly to do with winning games, with his ten per cent. But to understand the nature of Wenger's spats with Ferguson, it's important to show that Wenger has his own particular way of presenting himself to the media.

He did not, for a start, join its ranks, at least not in England. Wenger was never tempted by offers to enter the television studio and pontificate on matches that did not concern him. The senior managers, the old hands, they've all done their punditry on the burgeoning array of sports broadcast outlets: Keegan, Venables, Graham, Robson, Royle, Redknapp, Gullit, Dalglish, Hoddle, Souness, even Ferguson. But not Wenger. He was never a joiner-in anywhere. He was not, to use a male approval-word, clubbable. His default setting was silence, watchfulness, a certain distance, a mistrust of those he did not know, and had been ever since the day when, as a gangly teenager, he first fell in with footballers from outside his home village of Duttlenheim.

This tendency extends beyond his dealings with the media. 'At some point every manager will try to be the players' mate,' says Lee Dixon, 'play a round of golf, join in with a five-a-side game. George did. But Arsène never came to golf, never joined in the football. He's not that kind of man. In fact, I don't think Arsène is interested in being liked by his players. His wife comes to games and his daughter, too. But his family life is separate.'

In 1997 Wenger, who is not in fact married to his partner, bought a house round the corner from the Deins in Totteridge, and they socialise in each other's homes, but Wenger and his family trespass only rarely into the heart of the city where they settled.

Early on, Wenger established that he would not have individual relationships with members of the print media. He would not do one-on-one interviews with English newspaper journalists. He would not, it turned out, even refer to any of them by their names.

His post-match assessments for the most part find him hiding behind a narrow set of stock phrases that do scant justice to his command of the language. His utterances are not quite as inscrutable as the gnomic Nordic pseudo-profundities of Sven Goran Eriksson, another taciturn European in specs, who got the job of national coach after Wenger had proved that foreign coaches could succeed in England. Eriksson beguiled everyone with his ability to invest the phrase 'And of course that is good' with fathoms-deep resonance. Routinely Wenger will praise his players for their 'spirit', their 'qualities', explain that such and such a performance proves that so and so is 'exceptional', note that the result shows that his players are 'strong'/'tired'/'together'.

Wenger's post-match press conferences mostly set the pulse racing when, as is frequently the case, a player of his is sent off: his Pavlovian response is to excuse it ('Sol is not a dirty player'), or regretfully explain that he simply didn't see the incident. He has had ample opportunities to tick off Vieira and Bergkamp for their frequent misdemeanours on the pitch, or Anelka and Petit for their petulance off it. But mostly he would refrain, while occasionally criticising the dirty play of other teams. There was a time when he called a Charlton Athletic player 'a cheat' after he had committed more fouls than anyone else in the Premiership. 'Just imagine what people would be saying now if that was an Arsenal player,' said Wenger.

His pre-match press conferences at London Colney are of a slightly different order. Here he is more relaxed, and often speaks beyond the deadline pre-scribed by the Arsenal press officer. There hasn't just been a match to wind him up, and this is where his use of English is at its best. It soon emerged that he was a phrase-maker, even an aphorist. 'He comes out with some marvellous phrases,' says Winter. 'He has a great ability to introduce colour to a sentence – describing Ronaldo as "the pepper in Real Madrid's sauce".' Once, in response to Anelka's spiralling financial demands, Wenger ventured a pithy dressing-down. 'I told the boy he can sleep in only one bed and eat only three meals a day.'

It didn't take Wenger long to understand that the gaze of the British media, and its ravenous hunger for fresh news, was more intense than anything he had encountered in France and Japan. It became apparent after about a year that the media invariably filleted his pronouncements for his thoughts on one of two sub-jects. The first was the indiscipline of his players, and the issues arising from them – 'bad' refereeing, 'unfair' FA hearings, 'harsh' bans. The second was Manchester United, and their manager Alex Ferguson. There was a simple reason for this. When Wenger didn't finish first, he finished second to Ferguson. No other club came near: Leeds, Chelsea, Liverpool, Newcastle – they all carried the bridal train, but never the bou-quet.

There's no doubt who started it. Ferguson's early warning system went off in the spring of 1997 when Wenger proposed the abolition of FA Cup replays. 'He has no experience of English football,' said Ferguson. 'He's come from Japan. And he's into

English football and he is now telling everybody in England how to organise their football. I think he should keep his mouth shut. Firmly shut.'

That set the tone. And the pattern. Wenger would say something, and Ferguson would react. Wenger would helpfully suggest that things be run in such a way that it would make it easier for clubs like his, full of internationals and fighting on three or four fronts for much of the season. It would light Ferguson's fuse every time. When in 2001 Manchester United were press-ganged by the FA into attending the World Club Championship in Brazil in order to support England's abortive bid to host the 2006 World Cup, they were forced to duck out of the FA Cup. Wenger dismissed the trip as a 'midwinter break'. Until their participation was confirmed, Ferguson noted that several clubs had been grumbling. "The rest got on with their business once the decision was irrevocable but not Arsenal or their manager.'

And then there was Wenger's suggestion that it was far harder for Arsenal to win the Premiership than Manchester United because in the capital there were more local derbies. (Adams backs this one up: 'If we weren't in London,' he says, 'we'd have whipped this league. Man United's success has coincided with Man City going down. They've got no opposition whatsoever.')

'When I read that,' said Ferguson, 'I had to think it was some kind of joke. How does he define United-Liverpool or United-Leeds?'

Only in times of extreme tension can the boot be persuaded on to the other foot. In the championship run-in in the spring of 1999, Arsenal were seven points behind United and even sitting third behind Chelsea when the two clubs in front of them drew an FA Cup quarter-final and had to play each other again. 'Arsenal are probably in the best position to win the championship after this,' said Ferguson.

'Is that his latest joke?' said Wenger. 'Would he like to swap positions with us?' In each case, the attempt by one to claim that the other occupies a position of advantage is greeted by the same response: he must be joking. Wenger once described their sparring as 'a little bit of comedy'.

It was evident from the start that Ferguson was baffled by the culturally alien figure that Wenger embodies, with his university degree and his languages, his urbanity and his apparent absence of passion. Ferguson is also well read, with a knowledge of fine wines, and he found it hard to stomach that, next to this effete campus lecturer (who appears not to drink, at least not with him), he was caricatured as a fulminating dockyard bruiser. 'Intelligence!' he said in early 2003. 'They say he is an intelligent man, right? Speaks *five languages*. I've got a 15-year-old boy from the Ivory Coast who speaks five languages.'

Ferguson's attitude to Wenger is in part characterised by what could be seen as plain resentment. All English football was charmed, even seduced by this man who could reverse 70 years of dour footballing habits at Highbury in three weeks, and win a Double in less than two years. (Something similar happened with Eriksson's England team.) Ferguson started to behave like the local dreamboat when a handsome stranger pulls into town. He'd never had a real rival before, unless you count the over-emotional Kevin Keegan, whose spine he brutishly pummelled in one title run-in. He never got on with Kenny Dalglish much either. 'You'll get more sense out of this baby,' his fellow Scot once said, a grandchild in his arms, after some broadside or other from Ferguson. The difference with Wenger was he was new, and enigmatic, even exotic (back then English football still had enough of an island mentality to see foreign talent as exotic). Also, he stuck around, unlike Keegan and Dalglish, the serial quitters. And infuriatingly for Ferguson, his weapon of choice was one that the Glaswegian had not come across before. Wenger fought fire with ice.

It is dry ice, of course. Or irony. The oblique, deftly worded put-down. The most famous of these was in the spring of 2002. It has become a point of honour between these two men to claim that, if they finish as runner-up, they have nonetheless played the better football, while if they win they claim that the league table never lies. In 2002 it was Ferguson's turn to come second. 'We have played the best football in England,' he said, 'scored the most goals.' Wenger's off-the-cuff retort was Wildean in its deftness. 'Everyone,' he said, 'thinks they have the prettiest wife at home.' Ferguson was sufficiently unversed in the slippery ways of metaphor to take this as an *ad feminam* attack on his missus.

The pattern of these exchanges is that Ferguson does his best to get Wenger's attention and Wenger, who is by nature reticent and self-assured, does his best to withhold it. 'He doesn't bother me,' Wenger said in November 1997. 'Perhaps the more sensitive can be affected. I understand his passion and if I get under his skin then that is good.' In 2001, when United won the Premiership by 18 clear points, it irked Ferguson that Wenger, unlike other managers, did not honour the manly code in which the loser proffers his congratulations.

'I'll just have to accept,' said Ferguson in his autobiography, more in sorrow than anger, 'that between Old Trafford and Highbury appreciation is pretty much a one-way street.' Loftily, he added, 'I don't think his carping has made a good impression on other managers.'

Wenger inserts further distance between himself and Ferguson by speaking in a different idiom. Ferguson is blunt. Wenger is sharp. Ferguson is literal. Wenger is ellyptical. When asked once by reporters why he never drinks after games at Old Trafford, Wenger produced a classically sly evasion. 'I prefer wine to whisky.' This went straight back to Ferguson, who took him at his word. He told the press he'd get wine in.

It seems to surprise people that Wenger is funny. He looks deadly serious. He mostly sounds serious. And yet those who know him well swear by his sense of humour. 'The responsibility of his job makes him seem very serious,' says Jean-Luc Arribart, a friend since they played for the French students in the 1970s, and a player of Wenger's at Nancy. 'He cuts this quite severe figure, but he's very very funny. He really loves to laugh.'

At one charity dinner attended by both Dein and Gérard Houllier, Wenger was asked how good a footballer he was. 'I was the best,' he said. And then after a perfect pause, he added, 'In my village.'

And yet, however witty Wenger is with the press, among his own players the joke is often at his expense. He has the physical clumsiness that comes with living so thoroughly in his own head. 'You can bet that, if [hotel staff] have to partition off a ballroom for us, he will be the one to lean against the divider and knock it down,' says David Seaman in *Safe Hands*. 'Or he will be bent over his shoelaces when the door opens on his head.'

'He makes us laugh by the silly things that he does,' says Adams. 'He's forever tripping up and hitting his head and smashing things. He's got a plate of jellied dessert, he's turned round to talk to someone and and it's fallen off and he's looked back. "Where is my dessert?" He does that all the time. If he is sitting in a row of seats, he's got up and the other lot have fallen over. We are playing Crystal Palace. He's gone to the toilet, we've gone out, there is a bomb in the stadium and we've had to come back in. Arsène is coming out, doing himself up. "What is this?" Ray Parlour has gone, "There is a beumb in the stadium." "A beumb?" Everyone is on the floor at this stage. Ray Parlour has gone, "Yes, there is a beumb and there is an officer of the lieu coming into the dressing-room." "Raymond, are you taking the mickey out of me?" He laughs at things like that.'

This sense of fun was evident whenever he was called upon to comment on Ferguson. The BBC broadcaster Garry Richardson was interviewing Wenger for *Sportsweek*, his Sunday-morning show on Radio Five Live. 'I said something like, "Now, Alex Ferguson…" As soon as I said it Wenger said, "Oh yes, so what's he done now?" And he smiled. It was a cheeky smile. As much as to say, "Here comes a question about Fergie."'

His tendency was to view Ferguson as a naughty schoolboy. As Arsenal homed in on the Double in 2002, Ferguson attacked reporters who had criticised his purchase of Juan Sebastian Verón. His actual words were, minus expletives, reproduced in the newspapers. 'He's a f****** great player' and 'Youse are all f****** idiots.'

'What are all these asterisks in the newspaper?' Wenger asked reporters.

Before the 2003 Cup final he was asked to comment on the vexed question of who had played the better football in the Premiership – the winners or the runners-up. He smiled broadly. 'You want to put me in a controversial situation with Manchester United! I don't mind! I can live with that!' He certainly can. United sold David Beckham a couple of months later. It may have been the summer holidays, but Wenger was ready with his suggestion that United's outstanding group of youth-team graduates was now beginning to break up. 'The personal problems between Beckham and Ferguson,' he concluded, 'certainly lowered the fee,' before adding that United's greater financial clout would ensure that 'Manchester will lead the way in England now.' It was the usual trick: ceding ground in order to gain it.

'There is a real mischief-maker in him,' says Winter. 'He knows that he has got spectacularly underneath Ferguson's skin. Every time Ferguson talks about Wenger the temperature in the room changes. Wenger knows that he can make little prognostications and it will travel straight back into the heart of Ferguson's control room at Carrington [the Manchester United training ground]. Obviously the conduit for that is the media, so that is why Wenger likes to use the journalists to just needle him a little bit.'

There was another magisterial dressing-down in early 1999. Ferguson advised a small group of Sunday writers that Arsenal, who were champions at the time, liked 'a scrap'. Their style of play was 'belligerent'. 'The number of fights involving Arsenal,' he said, 'is more than Wimbledon had in their heyday.' So Wenger took the opportunity to insult Ferguson while loftily pretending that there was in fact nothing to respond to. 'What he said does not bother me at all and I do not want to make a fuss about it,' he said. 'I think it was just a little bit clumsy on his part.' Ferguson then issued his customary recantation, in which he absolved himself from blame while shooting the messengers, the reporters. 'Arsène Wenger has a right to be annoyed over this matter. I have already dropped him a note explaining the situation and I offered him the apology he deserved. It is not my policy to criticise teams and the way they play. People go on about it all being psychological warfare, but that is far from the truth on this occasion. I was stitched up and feel I have been betrayed.' But Ferguson did not apparently know the Highbury postcode. 'If he has written the letter,' said Wenger, 'it must have been sent by horse because I haven't received it.' It was as if the headmaster was indulging a school rebel for not handing his homework in on time.

'The great thing about him,' says Winter, 'and where he really differs from Ferguson, is if he says something which he knows is going to be controversial, he will never backtrack. He will never say, "That last bit was off the record." Whereas Fergie will have a rant about Arsenal's discipline and then say, "Aye, that was all off the record, don't use that." Wenger is very happy to be quoted.'

This is corroborated by another respected broadcaster. 'The great thing is you know Arsène Wenger isn't going to get up and storm out even when you asked the tricky question. If you want to say to him, "Are you worried about losing your job?" or "Are you going to sign Beckham?" you know you can ask that and he won't fly off the deep end. Whereas Alex Ferguson, if you ask him anything more than "Do Manchester United wear red shirts?" and "Is the ground called Old Trafford?" you are treading on dodgy ground and likely to get the hair-dryer treatment.'

In May 2003 another letter was never received, and in this case not even written. After United had won the title, Arsenal were preparing for the FA Cup final against Southampton. It was noted that Wenger had not written to Ferguson to congratulate him on his title. When the occasion arose, this was something Ferguson always did. 'I am not a great writer,' Wenger explained.

But he could put pen to paper. When Anthony Holden dedicated his third biography of Prince Charles to Wenger and the 1998 squad, he sent the chief dedicatee a copy. 'I got a witty letter back,' says Holden. 'I was surprised by how chuffed he seemed about a dedication in a book about a British prince. They were about to go off to a key European away game that year. There was some charming phrase: "If you see me reading the book in the dug-out during the match, you should be worried."' He also wrote to Laurence Marks, who had interviewed him for a book about Arsenal, that 'he was thrilled with the book and would read it as soon as possible'. (Wenger is a great reader of biographies, especially on long flights home from European games.)

There was one obvious reason why Wenger seemed to be less needled by Ferguson than the other way round. If it was a rivalry, for Wenger it was a big improvement on his last one, when he was at Monaco and Olympique Marseille were bribing their way unpunished to title after title. Ferguson is cussed, he is grouchy, he is sneaky and hypocritical ('Arsenal bullied the referee'!), he is occasionally plain rude. But he did not run a club which bribes opponents to throw games. He did not have a president phoning up key opposition players before big games to say, 'We're thinking of buying you in the summer.' None of Wenger's players was secretly conceding penalties to ease United's path to the championship. The playing-field was not quite level, because until they moved into the new stadium at Ashburton Grove, at each home game Arsenal played in front of 29,000 fewer paying spectators than Manchester United. But there were no illegalities involved. Once each club had emptied their wallets over the summer, for Wenger it was simply a question of pitting his wits against Ferguson's. Simply, the rivalry exercised Ferguson more because he hadn't had one like it. For Wenger, bribes and games thrown will break his bones, but names will never hurt him.

But there was another less obvious reason why one man was more adversarial than the other. As the two clubs fought for the Premiership in April 2003, writing in *The Guardian* the psychoanalyst Oliver James ascribed their contrasting behaviour, mainly in relation to each other, to seeds sown in childhood. Ferguson, he argued, was brought up in the school of literally hard knocks on the shipyard culture of the Clyde.

'His childhood will have left him expecting to be attacked and the interesting thing is the extent to which our early experiences still govern our adult expectations. Recent studies suggest we will provoke or manipulate people to behave in ways that conform with our childhood experiences. If little Ferguson was forever liable to be attacked, then trying to pick verbal fights could be his way of making the present familiar. Almost certainly, Ferguson sees Wenger as someone who is a threat and needs to be outwitted. But on top of that, deep down Ferguson probably sees the Frenchman as a weak, effeminate, duplicitous "bad" person who needs to be taught a lesson in the importance of discipline.'

There is one flaw in James's theory. He admits that

little is known of Wenger's childhood experiences. 'However', he adds, 'there is every reason to think they were not as traumatic as Ferguson's. To judge by his reactions to his rival's provocations, he is not easily made paranoid, suggesting he was not the object of much aggression.'

Wenger himself suggested in the 2003 run-in that he did not have 'a gift for paranoia'. Far from having an authoritarian for a father, Wenger was often left to his own devices in Duttlenheim, as his parents ran La Couronne d'Or, and, perhaps to fill the hole left by his hard-working father, went on to form strong bonds with men older than himself, including Max Hild at Mutzig, Aldo Platini at Nancy and Henri Biancheri at Monaco. He had, he later said, 'a kibbutz upbringing'. This was presumably the breeding ground for his reserve and his self-reliance.

And then came Ferguson's decision not to retire, halfway through what was planned as his valedictory season. Arsenal won the Double, and Manchester United won nothing. This concatenation of events seemed to trigger something in Wenger. He became super-confident. Rashly, he started making hostages to fortune. In the run-in, he said he was 100 per cent certain that Arsenal would win the title. 'The table doesn't lie,' he said. 'It's always right.'

A second Double, and Ferguson's vacillation, imbued him with a new certainty, even a new arrogance. It was as if Ferguson's U-turn had wiped the slate clean, had redrawn the lines. In his own mind, Wenger was moving into the superior room. By the start of the new season Wenger was predicting that in the following season, 'Nobody will finish above us. Our challenge is to dominate English football. I said that straight after winning the league at Old Trafford and many people thought I was a bit arrogant or pretentious. I just wanted to show how we don't want this to be a unique achievement.' He even declared that there had been a shift in power down to London.

If Wenger were to win again in 2003, it would be 3-3: three titles each in his six full seasons of going head to head with Ferguson. His team backed up his splendid prognosis by playing football of a quality that had an entire continent drooling at the prospect of a Champions League final between Arsenal and Real Madrid. There was the usual autumnal hiccup. Four games were lost in a row, including the one against Auxerre on Wenger's 53th birthday, prompting him to lock himself in his office and refuse David Dein's entreaties to join a party at San Daniele. But something went more seriously wrong in the spring. Arsenal started failing to hold on to leads. In the second phase of the Champions League, Henry scored a sublime hat trick in Rome, only for Arsenal to draw their other five games in the group.

Ferguson thought he knew the answer. 'Over-confidence is a failure in people and there is no doubt about it: they are over-confident. When you are that full of yourself – as Arsenal are – it can come back to haunt you. It is a dangerous game and you wouldn't catch us acting like that.'

In two months, from the start of March to the start of May, Arsenal saw an eight-point Premiership lead converted into an eight-point deficit. Halfway through April, United visited Highbury and Ferguson gave the knife another twist. 'The comments they made could come back to haunt them. It would be a terrible blow for Arsenal if we were top of the league after this game.' There was never any doubt that when he said 'they' he meant 'he'. In a soap opera of a game, the teams drew 2-2. The equaliser, a free header for Giggs a minute after Arsenal had taken the lead, sent Wenger into paroxysms of frenzy on the touchline. It was the most flustered that he had ever been in public. Ferguson also did something he never does, even if it wasn't quite out of character. He trespassed ostentatiously onto the turf to applaud the United fans. It was a calculated one-man pitch invasion, like one stag venturing onto another's urine-marked territory.

Before the end, Campbell was sent off for elbowing, and after Wenger lodged an appeal Ferguson hit Wenger right in the Achilles heel. 'The FA have to take action, and not reneging [on Campbell's four-match suspension] would be a start. Arsenal should be looking at their own man for doing something as stupid as that. We could have had a player with a broken nose or jaw, or serious eye injury because of his needless action.' The football correspondents had long joked that they would present Wenger with a clock on the occasion of the 50th Arsenal dismissal in his tenure. Campbell was the 49th.

As the dream of an unprecedented double Double faded, Wenger ran the risk of looking like a bad loser. After Arsenal's latest elimination from the Champions League, Manchester United went on to have a pulsating quarter-final with Real Madrid. 'Over 180 minutes,' Wenger said, 'you can say that Manchester United were never in a position to qualify. Not for one minute.' Then Thierry Henry won the Player of the Year award, ahead of United's Ruud van Nistelrooy, who won the Golden Boot.

'I think he got the biggest reward, the Player of the Year, for an individual player, and that's much more than the Golden Boot.'

The title was surrendered at home to Leeds, and Wenger embarked on a passionate display of wailing and gnashing of teeth. 'I have dropped every bit of blood and energy to fight for first place. I would be the proudest man in the world if we had won.' A year earlier Wenger had said that the table never lies. Now, apparently, it did. 'I still think if you look at the championship and the FA Cup we are certainly the best team but Manchester United found their form at the right moment.'

That summer, while Manchester United spent £30 million on new players and Chelsea, now owned by Roman Abramovich, splashed out £100 million, Wenger culled a huge number of players from his squad. Of the 22 who left, admittedly few were close to the first team, but among them were three significant names: Sylvain Wiltord, who as the club's record signing had spent three years proving that Wenger was not good at throwing money around; Martin Keown, the last of the defence inherited from George Graham, who retired; and Nwankwo Kanu, the rangy and talismanic Nigerian supersub. It was hardly a promising preamble for what was about to happen.

The team which became known as the Invincibles had already lost the habit of losing away in their previous championship season. In all they went 22 games without defeat. Another extraordinary record found them scoring in 47 consecutive games. Wenger started talking about what he called the 'not impossible' – to play a whole league campaign without losing a game. 'I can't see why it's so shocking to say it. Do you think Manchester United, Liverpool or Chelsea don't dream that as well? They're exactly the same. They just don't say it because they're scared to look ridiculous, but nobody is ridiculous in this job as we know anything can happen.' He could hardly cite the example of Preston North End, who had done it in the reign of Queen Victoria with only 11 teams to play.

The season started promisingly with four straight wins. In the sixth game, a goalless visit to Old Trafford, Van Nistelrooy missed a penalty in the final minute and those with a nose for omens might have intuited that there was something in the air. The autumn brought home wins over Chelsea and Spurs, and dogged away draws at the likes of Leicester and Bolton, clubs where things could always go wrong for Arsenal. They entered January of 2004 with a new striker signed in the transfer window – Juan Antonio Reyes. In February they passed George Graham's club record of 24 league games without defeat while Henry scored his 100th Premier League goal and they ended the month nine points clear. A draw at home to Manchester United found Ferguson conceding the championship in the manner of someone hoping to induce complacency in his rivals. 'They'll go on to win the league now – I'm sure of that. They are playing with great determination... a very strong team, so should win the league really.' The draw set a new record for games without defeat from the start of the season: 30.

It's not as if there weren't distractions: Arsenal reached the semi-final of both domestic cups and were knocked out of the Champions League quarter-final by Abramovich's Chelsea. One week in early April they exited both Europe and the FA Cup, but after thrashing Liverpool and Leeds at home (with seven more goals for Henry) they went to Tottenham on 25 April in a position to win Wenger's third title. Thanks to a last minute goal by Alan Shearer against Manchester United, Arsenal were able to celebrate in the home of their oldest enemy. There were two jittery draws and a nervy win before Leicester supplied the opposition for the last game. Vieira, Wenger's quintessential representative on the pitch, scored the winner, much as his indomitable captain Adams had charged forward to crown the 1998 championship win with a thumping left-foot drive.

Of all the things that were remarkable about the march of the Invincibles, perhaps the most remarkable is the fact that not once in 38 games – featuring 26 wins and 12 draws – were Arsenal behind with 20 minutes to go. It was a testament to the defence Wenger had built, featuring young, fast, dynamic ballplayers in his own image – Lauren, Campbell, Touré and Cole.

Even before it had been completed, Wenger suggested that it would never be done again. His greatest feat was to cast a long shadow.

VINCIBLE

'If I go into a season and I say, "For fuck's sake, if we don't win anything, they [the club's star players] will all leave," I have already lost. The problem of the media is always to imagine the worst and the problem of the manager is always to imagine the best. There is always a difference of thinking.'

Arsène Wenger

Arsenal's record run of 49 Premiership games without defeat ended, inevitably, at Old Trafford. It was met, just as inevitably, by grumbles from Arsène Wenger about the refereeing and, less predictably, by an unseemly post-match kerfuffle in the tunnel in which a dough-pasted refreshment was flung out of the Arsenal changing room – possibly by Cesc Fàbregas – and came to land on the person of Sir Alex Ferguson. 'This slice of pizza came flying over my head and hit Fergie straight in the mush,' recalled Ashley Cole. 'All mouths gawped to see this pizza slip off this famous, puce face and roll down his nice black suit.'

It may have been funny at the time, but Pizzagate was to cast a long shadow over Wenger's relationship with his old rival. They barely spoke for the next five years. According to Ferguson, Sunday 24 October 2004 proved a watershed in Wenger's managerial career. It 'scrambled Arsène's brain'. Wenger certainly harrumphed that he would not 'answer another question about this man'. And yet they still spoke supportively of each other. Later that season Wenger expressed his contempt for Manchester United fans who had taken to booing Ferguson as the club trailed in third place, and Ferguson often condemned United fans' chants referring to Wenger's entirely fictional sexual preferences. Nine years after the event, when Ferguson published an autobiography following his retirement, Wenger was asked again about Pizzagate and he dismissed it as 'a little unrest in the corridor after the 49th game', which suggested that, if nothing else, his ability to count had indeed been scrambled: the 2-0 defeat was the 50th game. He could still recall that Rio Ferdinand should have been sent off.

Arsenal instantly lost momentum. This would not be the last time Wenger's charges found themselves tripped up by a single reverse and plunged into a morale-sapping run at a crucial juncture. It would happen after Eduardo da Silva's leg was hideously broken at Birmingham in 2008 when Arsenal were five points clear, prompting Wenger to call for a life ban for the culprit (which he swiftly retracted). It happened again in 2010 when, as overwhelming favourites against the same opponents in the League Cup final, defeat caused their pursuit of three cups to come grinding to a halt.

But for the new vulnerability of the Invincibles, there were other factors in play. Even if they weren't talking, after Pizzagate the two old foes now had a common foe not given to mincing his words. José Mourinho was hired as Chelsea's new manager a year after Roman Abramovich took possession of the club. He had just won the Champions League with Porto, defeating Wenger's old club Monaco in the final. In his first press conference in England this notch on his belt enabled Mourinho bashfully to describe himself as 'a special one'. The epithet stuck. Mourinho's first championship was underwritten by Abramovich's casual disdain for the bottom line, the antithesis of everything Wenger stood for. He may not have been answering questions about Ferguson but Wenger was soon favouring the new young pretender with special attention in his weekly press conferences, commenting minutely on Chelsea's form. There was a clear spur for Wenger's anguish about the rise of Chelsea. The concept of the high-rolling neighbour was familiar to him from his years at Monaco when Bernard Tapie spent his way to five titles in a row. Mourinho did not like the tone of Wenger's attention. 'I think he is one of these – how do you call it – voyeurs,' he mused in October 2005. This was in response to a misreported comment of Wenger's about Chelsea's recent performances. 'He is someone who likes to watch other people. There are some guys who have this big telescope to see what happens in other families. He must be one of them. He speaks and he speaks and he speaks about Chelsea. He is always speaking about other families. Being a voyeur is a sickness.'

It was quite the rudest thing any other manager had ever said about Wenger, and he considered suing.

'When you give success to stupid people,' he said, 'it makes them more stupid sometimes.' Unfortunately for Wenger, the legal fees were also too much. 'Have you seen the price of lawyers in England?' he remarked. 'They say "Hello" and it's £100,000 before they shake your hand.' Less than a month later Chelsea consigned Arsenal to their third consecutive league defeat, a first under Wenger.

Mourinho's expensively assembled Chelsea side won the title, and then won it again, and then twice finished second to Manchester United. By then Mourinho had gone, to be replaced by a farcically long line of successors until he re-entered in 2013. But he was the catalyst causing Arsenal's unseating as England's second club. From 2005-6 onwards until Mourinho returned, Arsenal would finish fourth more often than third. They simply stopped winning things.

Even the 2005 FA Cup was eked out on penalties (setting an historic precedent) after the first final since 1912 ended without a goal. The opponents were Manchester United, who had beaten them two further times that season after the 49th game, including a bruising 4-2 at Highbury. Both clubs came into the final knowing this was their own chance of a trophy that season. 'Every day you read that you have not won anything and you cannot keep people happy unless you do that,' said Wenger. Thierry Henry was injured and, without him, the team resembled a dreadful throwback to George Graham's boring boring Arsenal. Bergkamp, playing as a lone striker, spent the afternoon on what may as well have been a desert island. 'I went for a more cautious approach on this one day,' said Wenger, 'to get what we wanted at any price. But I'm not convinced that you always have to play like that.' The performance was grim but still it prompted talk from David Dein of offering Wenger a job at Arsenal for life. Nearly a decade later with no further trophies to parade through the streets of Islington, that ugly final had somehow become the stuff of sepia-tinted nostalgia. Neatly symbolising the termination of an era, Vieira's winning penalty was his last kick as an Arsenal player.

So what happened?

Essentially the Emirates happened. Even as the Invincibles had turned Highbury into a fortress, a consensus spread throughout the club that a larger stadium delivering greater revenues was necessary for Arsenal's long-term ability to compete. This was a frequent refrain of Wenger's. Wembley, Arsenal's Champions League home from home for two seasons, was considered as an option before it too was razed and, over seven years, rebuilt. A brownfield site within a stone's throw of Highbury was found at Ashburton Grove and a new stadium duly climbed into the North London skyline.

Much as he had with London Colney, Wenger put his personal signature on the design of those parts of the stadium which impacted on the health and focus of his players. A drive-in tunnel kept them away from the distraction of autograph-seeking supporters on match day. The perimeter and tunnel were both widened from the narrow proportions of Highbury. A home dressing room with benches laid out in the

JASPER REES

shape of a horseshoe made Wenger the focus of team talks. And naturally all the trimmings of the training centre were matched.

But unlike London Colney, paid for entirely by the sale of Nicolas Anelka to Real Madrid, this was not going to be funded by realising the cash value of footballers. The story of the stadium's creation has been unimprovably told by Alex Fynn and Kevin Whitcher in *Arsènal: The Making of a Modern Superclub*. The seismic narrative, involving grandiose property speculations and a profound redistribution of power in the boardroom, impacted specifically on Wenger's day job of producing a football team in two ways.

On a personal level, Wenger lost his friend and sponsor David Dein, the vice-chairman responsible for bringing him to Arsenal. Dein found himself marginalised when he opposed the move to Ashburton Grove and his calls to keep funds available for replenishing the squad went unheeded. He was edged out altogether in 2007 after unilaterally making overtures to American sports impresario Stan Kroenke, and he would later cement his alienation from the board by falling in with Russian billionaire investor Alisher Usmanov (an event which found Wenger keeping his distance: 'I don't want to be involved in a strategic struggle for shares because, basically, it's not my problem'). Wenger's first reaction to Dein's unseating was to ask if he too should resign in solidarity. Dein encouraged him to stay put. Wenger made all the right diplomatic noises as he walked the wire between professional pragmatism and personal loyalty. 'It is a sad day for Arsenal,' he said. 'It is a huge disappointment

225

because we worked very closely.' Within days, having demanded a reassurance from the board, Wenger was announcing that a director of football – someone empowered to take on Dein's work with transfers and contracts – would be anointed by him. Though a powerful expression of Wenger's seeming omnipotence within the club, the club has never appointed anyone with that job title.

But whoever was actually negotiating the deals, the more significant impact of the stadium was on Wenger's ability to compete in the transfer market. 'What is the point of moving into a beautiful new stadium if you don't fill it with fans and world-class players?' he said long before the move was made. Wherever the world-class players were going to come from, they wouldn't be conjured up with an extravagant wave of the cheque book. According to the managing director Keith Edelman there was money to spend in 2006, the year of the move, and this mantra would be chanted by the board more than once. But it was not spent on marquee signings: after the club paid £13 million for Sylvain Wiltord in 2000, there wasn't a signing of a comparable size for another eight years until Samir Nasri and, the following year, Andrei Arshavin were both bought for £12 million.

As ever the club was still involved in big transfers, only these involved the departure of top players. Increasingly, though, they were leaving at a time of their own choosing rather than Wenger's. After Henry's departure, a succession of players were rewarded with the armband as an inducement to commit to Arsenal, regardless of their suitability to the role. William Gallas was made captain soon after criticising the club's managerial policy, and was demoted a year later after this time criticising his teammates for lacking bravery. At the height of the civil conflict within his own squad, Wenger made light of the role of the armband. 'I don't believe too much in leadership,' he said. 'I believe more in good passing than a guy who jumps around with the hands in the air and plays the leader.' The captains apparently put a low premium on it too. The loyalty bribe was not enough to pin down Cesc Fàbregas or Robin van Persie who, along with Gaël Clichy and Alex Song, eventually left for the promise of bigger gains, both in silverware and in pieces of silver. In each case they all soon won championships with their next club. When in 2013-14 Arsenal embarked on their most successful start to the season in many years, they did so with their club captain Thomas Vermeulen confined to the bench.

If Wenger's aura of invincibility was shattered in the 50th game, it took another symbolic blow in 2006. Arsenal surmounted a trio of princely clubs – Ajax, Real Madrid and Juventus – before again winning ugly against Villareal in the semi-final to reach their first Champions League final. Victory was confidently predicted on the streets of Islington where yellow warning signs went up on lampposts advising of a parade on Thursday 18 May. In pursuit of that victory, at the hotel Wenger showed his players a video of migrating geese in flight, deploying teamwork to share the burden of leadership. By the time the squad got to the stadium the talk was of the perfect golf swing and the importance of the follow through. 'If you stop halfway, you lose,' he said, 'You are the best players, you deserve to be here – now go out there and win this.'

The last time an English team had contested the most prestigious European final in Paris was 1975 when Leeds United's hooligan fans ripped up the seating in the Parc des Princes. Wenger was at that game with his mentor Max Hild. This time, in the Stade de France, it was on the pitch that tempers frayed. The goalkeeper Lehmann was sent off in the 18th minute and Henry was aggressively policed by Barcelona defenders who, it was widely rumoured, would be his teammates by the following season. Campbell headed in Henry's free kick in the first half and in the second Henry squandered a chance to put Arsenal 2-0 ahead, but with deft substitutions the Catalans eventually cruised to victory with two late goals.

Afterwards Wenger chastised the referee (if not as fiercely as Henry, who that night committed to stay at Arsenal at £130,000 a week instead of joining the opposing team) while wearing the brave face of the loser. 'We got such a wonderful ovation from the crowd that I'm just as happy as if we'd won,' Wenger said. However adept he is at moving on from triumph, the suggestion that such a devastating defeat could be so easily overcome did not ring true. As he watched the Barcelona coach Frank Rijkaard take possession of the trophy, he attained the unwanted distinction of becoming the only manager to lose in the final of all three European competitions.

It was the end of the line for the Invincibles. Robert Pirès, taken off in the final to make way for a substitute goalkeeper, departed. So did Campbell and Cole. Dennis Bergkamp retired. Within another season, Henry, Freddie Ljungberg, Lauren and José Antonio Reyes were gone. It turned out to be Wenger's best shot of a Champions League title in an era which saw the club's English rivals all win it – Liverpool in 2005, Manchester United in 2008, Chelsea in 2012 (all of them also losing a final too, United to Barcelona twice), while Mourinho won it again with Internazionale in 2010. In 2010 Wenger conceded that his failure to win the Champions League with Arsenal was a cause of insomnia. This being the era in which English clubs dominated, more than once Arsenal found themselves falling short in an all-English two-legged dogfight. In 2004 they lost to Chelsea in the quarter finals, in 2008 to Liverpool after beating Milan. A year later they were beaten by Manchester United in the semi-final when, eleven minutes into the second leg, they were already 3-0 down. Wenger described this as 'the most disappointing night of my career'. Another bad habit in the Champions League was Arsenal's frequent failure to win the group and guarantee themselves an easier ride in the first knock-out round: in 2011 they ran into Barcelona (a year earlier, Lionel Messi's double brace of goals at the Nou Camp had Wenger comparing him to a computer game player), then Milan in 2012, where they were thrashed 4-0, their heaviest loss in European football. 'A disaster,' said Wenger, who had sent on Henry, back briefly on loan from New York, to no avail.

According to Milan coach Arrigo Sacchi this was 'the worst Arsenal side in ten years'. A year on, again having got no further than the last 16, the club was immolated at home by Bayern. Often finishing the Premiership in fourth place also required Wenger's squad to take on two extra qualifying games at the start of the season.

Elimination from the Champions League became an annual restatement of a self-evident truth, that Wenger's squad was simply not strong enough – either in the quality (a Wenger buzzword) of the players or, increasingly, in physical stamina – to compete much beyond March. His squads also became progressively younger and slighter and, above all, less assertive. It was telling that a side which played in the image of physically indomitable captains – Tony Adams then Patrick Vieira – saw its tariff of red cards dwindle. Where in Wenger's early years Arsenal would suffer five, six or seven dismissals per Premiership season, the figures slumped to three, two or (in a couple of seasons) one red card. Wenger's teams were becoming, on average, more polite. 'Don't worry,' Wenger said in 2008, 'the Arsenal player who jumps out of a tackle will get a bollocking from me.' But with Vieira and Gilberto Silva gone, and Mathieu Flamini going to Milan that same year, there were fewer players jumping into tackles let alone out of them. Instead Wenger's big egos tended towards querulousness and self-regard – the sacked captain Gallas, the walking argument Adebayor who in the 2007 League Cup final against Chelsea got himself sent off in a stoppage-time imbroglio ten minutes after coming on as a substitute tasked with scoring an equaliser. It was the wrong sort of aggression which for a time also sprouted in an ongoing feud between Wenger's two goalkeepers, Lehmann and Manuel Almunia.

In footballing terms it meant that, increasingly, there was only one way to goal, via the geometrical blizzard of passes by a hyper-mobile midfield. The template was borrowed from the all-conquering Barcelona and Spain. Wenger invoked the comparison himself in 2010 when the media, voicing the anxieties of many fans, asked him if he might consider a more direct style. 'It's the same when Barcelona plays,' he said. 'When they win everybody admires the way they play. When they don't win, everybody says, "Why don't you change your style?" I believe we have to play our real game but with more belief, be more dynamic instead of changing completely our style.' Fans may have talked purringly of Arsenalona, but Wenger didn't quite have the players to merit the comparison week in, week out. Less talented but more obdurate teams found they could thwart Arsenal's highly tuned thoroughbreds by packing the midfield and sapping the vulnerable morale of a team which was essentially leaderless. Hence the ignominy of defeat by Birmingham City in the League Cup Final. Hence the growing difficulty of landing any form of decisive blow on their rivals. Weeks before the Birmingham debacle, an 11th game without a win against Chelsea or Manchester United prompted Wenger to the bold step of blaming defeat on the state of the Old Trafford pitch. 'The pitch was so poor in my opinion and the game suffered a lot from it,' he said. 'I ask you, "Do you want a good pitch or a bad pitch?" What do you say?' If everyone thinks they have the prettiest wife at home, Wenger also thought he had the prettiest grass.

Of course with fewer players being sent off Wenger had less occasion to deploy his infuriating myopia. In 2009 he finally admitted that he sometimes pretended not to see fouls committed by his own players 'because you know you cannot explain it'. For all the improvement in his 20/20 vision, his body language was participating in another narrative altogether, in which intense frustration triggered involuntary twitches and random contortions. Wenger started to wear his heart on his sleeve, to snipe and carp and sulk and look for excuses. The impassive mask and the aloof demeanour characteristic of the early-period Wenger vanished. He also accumulated a series of touchline bans. After one such in 2010, for pushing an assistant referee, Wenger was described admiringly by Harry Redknapp as – though he didn't use these precise words – one of us. 'We can all remember when Arsène first came to England – I remember reading articles saying he was like a professor watching the game and all the other nutters were jumping up and down, shouting and screaming. And that he wasn't like these idiots, that he's studying every move that's going on on the pitch like chess... Now he's joined the nutters. In fact he's one of the key nutters.' In the birthplace of football, Arsène Wenger was going native.

'I cannot sit there and be placid like I am on dope,' Wenger conceded later in the same season. 'I care about the game and I'm motivated to win the game and agitated.' In the climactic period of the same season, Wenger ignited when van Persie was sent off against Barcelona – unjustly in the manager's view. His lambasting of the referee earned him an improper conduct charge from UEFA, the governing body which Wenger promptly dismissed as a 'dictatorship'.

While the limbs became erratic and the face ever more mobile, other evidence that the great brain may indeed have been scrambled surfaced in his blue-sky pontifications. Among the ideas Wenger has floated include the scrapping of the mid-season transfer window, vetting of UEFA referees, getting rid of the away-goals rule in Europe and, in one mad supremacist plan to keep the ball forever more on the floor, even proposing to ditch throw-ins. In 2014 he complained about the fixture list giving Arsenal less recovery time than any of their rivals. 'Wenger complaining is normal because he always does,' said Mourinho, now back at Chelsea. 'It's in his nature.'

Some of Wenger's pronouncements issued through the foghorn of the media are of course perfectly sensible, but this did not stop a fratricidal attack in 2008 from UEFA president Michel Platini. Already a critic of Arsenal's policy of signing pre-adult players from other countries, he took issue with Wenger's views on the sound financial management of football clubs and the use of video technology to assist referees. 'It would make me happy that Arsène Wenger never sees it,' Platini said. 'I like to talk about football, him about business. We must stop with Wenger and all that.' On this occasion Wenger had right on this side. 'I am for sporting justice and UEFA must be the guarantor of it,' he replied. 'I am a supporter of good management of clubs, for financial equilibrium. And UEFA must equally support this idea. I am fighting for the future of the game and of football. I don't see why UEFA should take umbrage at ideas that are different from theirs.' Umbrage was actually taken by Platini's father Aldo, who had given Wenger his first managerial job at Nancy. The chastened younger Platini swiftly admitted that he had gone too far. 'I have been scolded by my dad who gave him his first start.' But he allowed himself a last word. 'When I talk about business, I mean attracting young players aged 13 or 14. I can't bear that.'

The business model for Arsenal increasingly turned towards the development of youth. With much less money to spend on the sort of showy purchases made by richer rivals, Wenger's network of scouts scoured Europe, Africa and South America (but curiously not Japan) for young players who ticked all the relevant boxes: speed, skill, athleticism, strength. Over the years his commitment to youth development has not necessarily been of much use in the first team. Ashley Cole and Jack Wilshere are the two most notable graduates to have joined Arsenal at the start and worked their way up, while the likes of Fàbregas, Theo Walcott and Aaron Ramsey were bought as semi-raw teenagers and honed under Wenger.

These players were beneficiaries of Wenger's vast wisdom on diet and fitness, but his philosophies had long since percolated out across the Premiership and gave less of an advantage than it once had. In 2008 an intriguing document came to light which revealed how Wenger went the extra yard to motivate his players. 'A team is as strong as the relationships within it,' it explained. 'The driving force of a team is its member's [sic] ability to create and maintain excellent relationships within the team that can add an extra dimension and robustness to the team dynamic. This attitude can be used by our team to focus on the gratitude and the vitally important benefits that the team brings to our own lives. It can be used to strengthen and deepen the relationships with it and maximise the opportunities that await a strong and united team.' A series of bullet points went on to stress the need for 'a positive attitude on and off the pitch... an unshakeable belief that we can achieve our target... focus on being mentally stronger and always keep going until the end... the desire to win in all that you do.' This sort of literature wasn't available to the squad at Bolton Wanderers. But then its precepts wouldn't have needed spelling out for Wenger's title-winning teams which Adams and Vieira led by example.

As season after season the dust gathered in the Emirates' empty trophy cabinet, fans complained about the money left unspent in the club bank account – sometimes as much as £80 million. In 2010, sounding an aggrieved note in his weekly press conference, Wenger drew attention to his exemplary record in youth development. 'One day I'll give you the list of those at the top level who have made careers with me and you will see. You will be absolutely astonished. I don't make any list but when I meet someone and think, "Oh, he started with me," then you see... If you go back, it is unbelievable the number of players who started at this club.' He didn't list the vast majority of kids under his wing who tend not to make it and end up being sold on. The stars of the future who were unable to repay Wenger's faith in them would scatter across the globe to clubs such as Ascoli, Atlético Paranaense, SC Preußen Münster, Buriram United, not to mention Dagenham and Redbridge.

The strategy for nurturing youth was laid out at the start of September 2007, the same week that Dein sold his stake in the club to the Russian investor Usmanov for £75 million. Wenger essentially said he didn't need an influx of foreign money, at least in the short term. 'You have to see how the game's evolution is in the next four or five years. But if I wanted to buy a player today I have money available. Will I need it in four or five years? I don't know. Maybe it depends on how much money all the other clubs have and what the average salary is. But self-sufficiency should be any club's target. You cannot have a policy at the club that, every year, somebody puts £50m or £100m in. Prices are rising but will people continue to pump in £40m, £50m or £100m every year without any natural resources or dividends paid back? I'm not convinced. You have to work with a club's natural resources. There is no other way. You will not find people for the next 25 years prepared to pump £50m or £100m into a club. That cannot work.'

This was the Strasbourg economics graduate speaking. But Wenger's fear of foreign money – what might be termed oligarchophobia – was ideological. And it would be borne out as many Premiership clubs fell into the clutches of owners, often ignorant of football culture, who proved irresponsible with debt – borrowing against the annual windfall from BSkyB – and insensitive to fans, proposing a change to shirt colours or club names. Wenger was protected from all this, and further insulated himself by keeping away from the high rollers luring big names to his Premiership rivals. He used the unlikely occasion of a Franco-British summit held at the Emirates in 2008 to outline a personal ideology of sound financial self-governance that he fervently wished to make law in the world of football. 'I don't feel any more in the modern world that there is a big difference between socialist or right wing,' he said. 'There is only one way to lead the world and that is to be as social as you can by surviving economically.' A year later Wenger was worrying that the global downturn and the weakening of the pound would dissuade foreign talent from coming to play in England. His rivals took an alternative view on profit and loss, even if none of the vast fees – ranging from £30 million to £50 million – paid for Andrei Shevchenko and Fernando Torres by Chelsea, Andy Carroll by Liverpool and Robinho by Manchester City would be justified by performances. More disturbing was the new world record paid by Real Madrid to lure Gareth Bale away from Spurs in the summer of 2013. The first €100 million transfer, which came in the same season UEFA introduced a rule designed to outlaw overspending, 'makes a joke of the financial fair play regulations,' said Wenger. 'I find it amazing that in the year the regulations come in, world football has gone completely crazy... It looks like it has made everybody worse than before.'

The landmarks came and went. 'I said to my wife I will stop at 50,' he said in October 2006, 'after I said at 55, and now I don't know...' This was on the occasion of the tenth anniversary of his arrival at the club, which was noted more by others than by Wenger himself. The same went for his 60th birthday on 22 October 2009, spent at the Arsenal AGM assuring shareholders that this looked certain to be the year the drought would end and faith in youth would at last be rewarded. As his squad grew younger and Wenger older, he claimed it was the players' potential which was keeping his mind sprightly. 'I am in a job where you always look in front of you. Unfortunately, the older you get, the less distance there is in front of you... This team keeps me young.' Contracts were renewed – in 2007, then in 2010 after Wenger conceded that this would be his last opportunity to leave. 'I am at the stage where if I extend my contract, it means I will finish my career at club level at Arsenal,' he said. 'If I go for a different challenge – I have been offered many challenges you know – it has to be now. That's a decision I have to make.' He signed.

Wenger's mantra was always to look forward. There is no trophy cabinet at home, no display case for the medals. 'I must have some but I don't know where they are,' he once said. His habit was to give them away, sometimes to his family, though the Champions League runners-up medal he didn't even bring home from the stadium in Paris. 'I don't know who has got it. I am not interested in that at all...

When I don't work anymore and I sit there living in the past, maybe I will try to put things together.'

This capacity to focus on the future allowed Wenger to survive a decade of frustration. Towards the start of every season he would once again declare that it was high time Arsenal won something, while in the same breath alluding to the spending power of rivals. The absence of trophies became a matter of growing urgency for the fans who paid more for even the cheapest season tickets than the most expensive ones almost anywhere else in England. It was in 2008/9 that the unthinkable notion began to form in the minds of a vocal minority – that Wenger should move on before Arsenal slipped any further. 'Football is not just like going to the supermarket,' he told the AGM that October. 'You can't go in and say, "I want one player who is six feet five inches with a good left foot."' It was in the light of growing restlessness on the terraces, and Arsenal's position as England's fourth best club under threat from Aston Villa, and the media imagining the possibility of Wenger being sacked, that Arshavin was lured from Zenit St Petersburg in the transfer window of January 2009. He made an instant difference until Wenger once more revealed his gathering disdain for domestic cup competition by omitting him from an FA Cup semi-final against Chelsea. The excuse was to prepare for the Champions League tie against Manchester United, for which the Russian was ineligible. They lost both encounters and – despite a 21-match unbeaten run - finished a humiliating 18 points behind United in the Premiership.

At an extra-plenary question-and-answer session a few weeks later Wenger was more or less ambushed by shareholders – that is, those fans whose allegiance to the club was such that they even owned a little piece of it. Wenger dealt with the onslaught a bit like his panicky defence. 'At the moment the vibes around the team are very negative,' he said, 'but I feel the Arsenal supporters should take a little distance from that, and not get manipulated too much.' Having told fans that they were having their heads turned by the media, he instructed them to behave more like supporters. 'What is important when you are a young team is to be supportive. It is easy to sit in the stand and say they are not up for the fight.' He left the meeting feeling deeply wounded. From now on there would be vetting of questions at all such gatherings.

Speculation erupted that Wenger would pick up his ball and take it to Real Madrid. His name had often been linked to that of the Spanish superpower but now, the day after the Q&A, he even described the notion as 'strongly interesting', and would not deny having met Real's returning president, Florentino Pérez. While he has often alluded to courtship from other clubs – 'I might write a book one day about all the contacts I have had,' he once said – there was no serious intention to leave. But he didn't baulk at scaring his critics. Nor did he show qualms about publicly licking his wounds. He suggested, for instance, that he much preferred the fans who travelled to away matches – 'who are absolutely fantastic' – rather than the ones who just went to the Emirates. 'You are in the last four in Europe, and every day you feel you have killed someone. It is unbelievable. If you do not take a distance with it, you think, "What kind of world do we live in?" We lose against Man United who have 10 times more resources, it's not a shame.' (The next time the clubs met Arsenal did lose and Wenger complained about Manchester United's aggressive tackling. Ferguson attributed it to anxiety about the empty trophy cabinet.)

Fourth became the new goal. In 2011 Arsenal were second from January to April but finished fourth. In 2012 they spent much of the second half of the season in sixth or fifth, before stealing up on Spurs to finish fourth. With lowered expectations, and the promise of success more or less permanently deferred, the atmosphere continued to be volatile in the babbling cyber-sphere occupied by blogging fans and all forms of media. A debate in the stands rumbled and roared about Wenger's continuing usefulness to the club: should he stay or should he go? Wenger became ever more thin-skinned. The AGM in 2012 – after the sale to Manchester United of van Persie, the source of 30 goals in the previous season – was again sour. Wenger was asked why he set such little store by the domestic cups. 'If you want to attract the best players,' he explained, 'they do not ask, "Did you win the League Cup?" They ask you, "Do you play in the Champions League?"' That season Arsenal were knocked out of the League Cup by Bradford and the FA Cup – at home – by Blackburn. At a press conference before Arsenal took on the mighty Bayern Munich in the last 16 of the Champions League, Wenger simmered with chippiness and paranoia after he was asked about extending his contract. 'I think I work for 16 years here in England and I deserve a bit more credit than wrong information that has only one intention is to harm.' Arsenal lost 3-1 at home. In the AGM later that year a new system was introduced in which questions were now displayed on a huge screen, muting potential shareholder unrest still further. 'We live in a society where everybody has an opinion on everything,' Wenger said at the start of the following season. 'I'm like somebody who flies a plane for 30 years and I have to accept that somebody can come into the cockpit and thinks he can fly the plane better than I do.' A few days later Arsenal were beaten 8-2 at Old Trafford. In all they let in 49 goals that season and finished 19 points behind the two Manchester clubs. 'I experience every defeat like a death,' he said at the start of the following season, and of no defeat can this have been truer.

For all the wonderful skills of Arsenal's next generation, one of the things that went missing after the Invincibles broke up was a solid defensive wall. Supporters waiting for Wenger's fourth great Arsenal team to form would grow used to the defence shipping goals in alarming quantities. The nadir was that hideous afternoon at Manchester United. 'We were very naïve defensively,' a shellshocked Wenger explained of his weakened side. A couple of years on there were six let in at Manchester City. Even if they carried on scoring at the other end, on several occasions Arsenal could be jittery about defending a lead. Three times in less than three years they contrived to score four and still draw the game. Harry Redknapp's first game in charge at Tottenham in October 2008 found Arsenal 4-2 up until the 89th minute. Six months later at Liverpool, Arshavin scored his fourth goal of the game in the last minute, only for Arsenal to let in an equaliser with the last kick. They were four up at Newcastle by half time in February of 2011, but in the second half let four in. Such scorelines cannot be considered a coincidence.

These things did not happen under George Graham, not with the defence he bequeathed to Wenger. The pairing of Campbell and Touré (moved to central defence from elsewhere on the park) continued the thou-shalt-not-pass tradition established by Adams, Bould and Keown. But overall Wenger seemed to have lost his eye for stoppers. Even Wenger concedes that defenders reach their peak later than players who do their work further up the field. With this longer gestation to full maturity, it is less clear which teenagers will develop reliably into the role. Among the names of centre backs who are less than fondly lauded in the club's history are Stepanovs, Cygan, Senderos, Silvestre, Squillaci. Several former Arsenal players, while clearing their throats with homages to the master, would make mildly dissenting noises in the media. In April 2012, with Arsenal running out of puff and the wheels already off for another season, Campbell suggested it was time for a change on the training pitch, recommending Bergkamp and Vieira as ideal coaches. But he was not hopeful. 'Arsène is a single-minded leader who does not like to have anyone around who could threaten his authority, either by challenging his decisions or by being the person that will eventually take his job. But hopefully he proves me wrong and makes such an appointment.' In May 2012 the retirement of Pat Rice, who had been with the club for 44 years, enabled Wenger to promote Steve Bould. The old virtues of defensive solidity which Bould embodied did not resurface immediately. But with the consolidation of a settled pairing of Per Mertesacker and Laurent Koscielny in the autumn of 2013, Wenger's perpetual promise of green shoots began to look as if it might mean something, despite the terrifying concession of six goals at Manchester City and five at Liverpool. A group of youngsters were now hitting their peak, including, for the first time in several seasons, a number of British players all schooled in Wenger's footballing philosophy of guile and speed and precision: Walcott, Gibbs, Wilshere, Ramsay and Alex Oxlade-Chamberlain. In that season he also gave a debut to the first player to be born since his arrival at Arsenal: Gedeon Zelalem, a gifted young 16-year-old midfielder whose nationality is a typically Wengerian stew of Somalian, German and American.

But there was another element to add to this source of optimism. In 2012 the Premier League published the net spending of its clubs over a five-year period. Predictably, Manchester City and Chelsea, both owned by foreign energy billionaires, came top, with a net spend of, respectively, £407 million and £232 million. (Oddly Stoke City trailed in a distant third on £75.2 million.) Eleven other clubs recorded a net loss. Of the six clubs which had turned a profit, Arsenal's was easily the largest at £45 million. Then Wenger splashed out almost all that on a single player.

Something shifted. Wenger spent the summer not trying and failing to buy big-name strikers such as Higuain, Suarez, Rooney and Benzema, and complaining at the silly money Tottenham were able to extract from Real Madrid for Gareth Bale. Just as fans were settling in to observe the formal commencement of the usual summer dance, it was announced that the brilliant German playmaker Mesut Özil would be coming to the Emirates. Thanks to the Bale signing he had been rationalised by Real and Wenger did the swift schmoozing necessary to keep him from the clutches of the Qatari-owned Paris Saint-Germain: he invited Özil to his home in Totteridge and was able to coax him aboard in German. Growing up in rural Alsace with Germany just the other side of the nearby Rhine had its upside.

By spending £42.5 million, at a stroke Arsenal leapt up the league table for record transfer expenditure on a single player by an English club. In England, only Chelsea have paid more – for Torres. It was the most visible sign yet that the Emirates Stadium was paying back on the investment. It also told Arsenal fans that Wenger is now alive to the reality that if he can't beat the sultans and oligarchs, he is going to have to join them. It's taken only ten years. Further way-stations loom: official retirement age of 65, ten years at the Emirates, a twentieth anniversary at Arsenal. Perhaps UEFA will even come good on its promise to punish clubs which, unlike Arsenal, breach its Financial Fair Play rules.

For Arsène Wenger, the economics graduate raised on football talk in a pub in Duttlenheim, the search for the elixir of success through youth, beauty and sound business principles goes on, and on, into the future where he has made his home. Once, when asked how long he'd stick around at Arsenal, he responded with a joke. 'I would love to be here forever,' he said, 'because that would make me immortal.'

GLOSSARY

A note on Arsène Wenger's English. At times in this book he will appear to speak what is (approximately) his fourth language more fluently and less idiosyncratically than at other times. This is because, on those occasions where he was originally speaking or writing in French (sometimes via Japanese), the quirks of his English have not been replicated in translation. In the chapter called 'Manager', for example, his pithy utterances to the English press are extensively quoted. But in the quotations which front each chapter, the words mostly started out in French.

I have translated French footballing terms wherever desirable. However, some words and phrases crop up in French. In English football, each club seems to have a different job title for its chief executive. David Dein, for example, is the vice-chairman of Arsenal. It's the same with two of Wenger's employers in France. Aldo Platini was the *directeur sportif* at AS Nancy Lorraine. Henri Biancheri remains the *directeur technique général* at Monaco. At AS Cannes Richard Conte was the *manager général*. In each case they have a president perched above them with overall financial control, so I've chosen to refer to them both as 'director of football'. In France the league title is known as the Championnat, and the main knockout competition as the Coupe de France. On the principle that we always refer to Serie A, the Bundesliga and the Primera Liga, I've kept the local French titles too. I refer to *les espoirs* on several occasions where I could more prosaically have used the term 'youth team'. Likewise, French football has a system in which each professional club has a *centre de formation*, which literally translates as 'training centre'. That dull phrase hardly begins to convey the function of a *centre de formation*, where a club's *espoirs* and reserves are grouped into a side which usually plays in the National, the equivalent of the third division, or possibly the upper tier of the Championnat de France Amateur (CFA), the equivalent of the fourth division. Both divisions have been structured in a variety of ways over the years. I've kept the French term to mirror the foreignness of the concept. Arsène Wenger had charge of two *centres de formation*, at Racing Club de Strasbourg and AS Cannes. AS, incidentally, stands for Association Sportive, although the term FC is also used in France – notably, at least where this book is concerned, by FC Duttlenheim and FC Mulhouse. Monaco, just to confuse things, is known as Association Sportive de Monaco Football Club.

Arsène Wenger is from Alsace. He is, therefore, *alsacien*. Or, as we don't often say, Alsatian. This caught me between a rock and a hard place. I could either use the French word with grating regularity, particularly in the first three chapters, or use a translation now wholly associated with a breed of dog favoured by the police. I plumped for option two in the hope that the reader get used to it.

A *cannonier* is a Gunner.

ACKNOWLEDGEMENTS

They are too numerous to list, but I am indebted to everyone who was interviewed for this book, particularly those who put up with my haltering French. Jean-Marc Guillou, Jean Petit and Richard Conte were tirelessly helpful long after the tape recorder had been turned off. My thanks to them for their generosity.

I would like to thank the following journalists and broadcasters: Xavier Rivoire, Jean-Marc Butterlin, Jean-Pierre Rivais, Eric Bielderman, Jeremy Walke, Gavin Hamilton, Jonathan Wilson, Michael Plastow, Pierre Hugonin, Ian Ridley, Henry Winter, Alyson Rudd, John Cross, Kevin Garside, Mark Pougatch, Garry Richardson and Alan Green. My thanks also to James Gill of United Agents and to Rebecca Nicolson and Paul Bougourd of Short Books.

Finally I would like to thank two old friends, not of mine, but of each other: Max Hild, for taking me to Duttlenheim, and Arsène Wenger, for not stopping him. But, as I discovered, that would have been out of character.

BIBLIOGRAPHY

Adams, Tony with Ridley Ian, *Addicted* (Willow, 1999)

Blair, Olivia and Flynn, Alex, *The Great Divide: Season 1999-2000 at Arsenal and Tottenham* (André Deutsch, 2000)

Cole, Ashley, *My Defence* (Headline, 2006)

Ferguson, Alex, *Managing My Life: My Autobiography* (Hodder & Stoughton, 2000)

Fynn, Alex and Whitcher, Kevin, *Arsènal: the Making of a Modern Superclub* (VSP, 2011)

Haynes, Alex, Ortelli, Daniel and Rivoire, Xavier, *The French Revolution: Ten Years of English Football after Cantona* (Mainstream, 2002)

Moffett, Sebastian, *Japanese Rules: Japan and the Beautiful Game* (Yellow Jersey, 2003)

Palmer, Myles, *The Professor: Arsène Wenger at Arsenal* (Virgin, 2001)

Pires, Robert, *Footballeur: An Autobiography* (Yellow Jersey, 2003)

Seaman, David, *Safe Hands: My Autobiography* (Orion, 2000)

Wenger, Arsène, *Shosha No Esprit* (NHK, 1997)

Jasper Rees's first football report (Bristol City 3 Chelsea 1) was the back-page lead in the launch edition of the *Independent on Sunday*. His other books are *Blizzard: Race to the Pole*, *I Found My Horn* and *Bred of Heaven*. He lives in west London.